how to be a
better....

project
manager

THE INDUSTRIAL SOCIETY

The Industrial Society stands for changing people's lives. In nearly eighty years of business, the Society has a unique record of transforming organisations by unlocking the potential of their people, bringing unswerving commitment to best practice and tempered by a mission to listen and learn from experience.

The Industrial Society's clear vision of ethics, excellence and learning at work has never been more important. Over 10,000 organisations, including most of the companies that are household names, benefit from corporate Society membership.

The Society works with these, and non-member organisations, in a variety of ways – consultancy, management and skills training, in-house and public courses, information services and multi-media publishing. All this with the single vision – to unlock the potential of people and organisations by promoting ethical standards, excellence and learning at work.

If you would like to know more about the Industrial Society please contact us.

The Industrial Society
48 Bryanston Square
London
W1H 7LN
Telephone 0171 262 2401

The Industrial Society is a Registered Charity No. 290003

how to be a better....
project
manager

Trevor L. Young

KOGAN PAGE   The Industrial Society

YOURS TO HAVE AND TO HOLD
BUT NOT TO COPY

First published in 1996
Reprinted 1997 (twice), 1998, 1999, 2001

Kogan Page Limited
120 Pentonville Road
London N1 9JN

© Trevor Young, 1996

British Library Cataloguing in Publication Data
A CIP record for this book is available from the British Library.
ISBN   0 7494 1945 8

Typeset by Photoprint, Torquay, Devon
Printed in England by Clays Ltd, St Ives plc

CONTENTS

HOW TO BE A BETTER . . . SERIES

Whether you are in a management position or aspiring to one, you are no doubt aware of the increasing need for self-improvement across a wide range of skills.

In recognition of this and sharing their commitment to management development at all levels, Kogan Page and the Industrial Society have joined forces to publish the How to be a Better ... series.

Designed specifically with your needs in mind, the series covers all the core skills you need to make your mark as a high-performing and effective manager.

Enhanced by mini case studies and step-by-step guidance, the books in the series are written by acknowledged experts who impart their advice in a practical way which encourages effective action.

Now you can bring your management skills up to scratch *and* give your career prospects a boost with the How to be a Better ... series!

Titles available are:

How to be Better at Giving Presentations
How to be a Better Problem Solver
How to be a Better Interviewer
How to be a Better Teambuilder
How to be Better at Motivating People
How to be a Better Decision Maker
How to be a Better Communicator
How to be a Better Negotiator
How to be a Better Project Manager

Available from all good booksellers. For further information on the series, please contact:

Kogan Page, 120 Pentonville Road, London N1 9JN
Tel: 0171 278 0433   Fax: 0171 837 6348

1

INTRODUCTION

Are you experiencing change in your everyday life? Of course you are because we are surrounded by change both at work and in our family life. As time moves inexorably on we are faced with new challenges every day as the changes impact on us. Some of these changes are created by personal choice that are usually under our control within certain economic constraints which we try to fix.

Other changes we face are not so selective. Changes in the way we live are often imposed on us by legislation, the government and our environment. Others are imposed on us at work by our employers and the managers who decide what we must do, when and how it must be done. Often our input is limited and we are expected to accept these changes without complaint in the interests of the organization.

We are also surrounded by change through the wide range of new products we are urged to buy through the advertising media. All these new products start out as a simple idea based on someone's creative ability. The idea must then be turned into reality which often involves many different skills being applied in an organized manner with a controlled timescale to get the new product on the market as soon as possible.

All of these changes have one thing in common – they have to be effectively managed by someone if they are to be successful. Change that is uncontrolled is subject to significant risk and potentially serious consequences for everyone and even the organization.

QUESTION

What changes have recently had an impact on you? Write down a short list and then ask yourself:

❑ How were these changes communicated to you?
❑ How were these changes designed and implemented?
❑ Were the consequences of the changes measured?
❑ Was there a reaction to the measurements made?

The process of managing change is important, from the initial idea through to controlling the consequences and reacting to any problems that occur. Success only comes from a strong commitment to this careful monitoring and continuous improvement. New products have little chance of success if there is no sales and marketing plan to promote and sell the product with good support, service and maintenance backup.

We can only achieve this success by following a series of carefully designed steps:

❑ understand the current situation;
❑ clearly state why the change is necessary now;
❑ identify some measurable benefits from the change;
❑ decide how the change is to be implemented;
❑ identify the possible consequences;
❑ communicate the process;
❑ implement the change;
❑ measure the benefits;
❑ respond promptly to the problems that arise;
❑ seek to continuously improve.

Each of these steps is achieved by using a specific set of skills and techniques that at work are usually associated with the role of a manager. Although major changes are often the responsibility of a manager, many are given to anyone who is considered to have the essential 'technical' knowledge and experience for the job. The vehicle that carries all these skills and techniques is the *project*. This is a convenient label to describe the collection of activities that creates the change process and reacts to the impact on people, the organization and, where appropriate, the customer and the market place. The project is concerned with creating change in an organized and structured manner.

HOW DOES THIS AFFECT YOU?

If you are given the responsibility for creating some change in your organization, you are faced with using these skills and techniques to achieve a successful result. You may already have some responsibility for people as a manager or you may be a member of a departmental team. The project has to be managed and the role is generally a temporary one, ranging from a few weeks or months to more than a year in duration. As the *project manager* you are expected to focus all or more usually just part of your time on achieving that success. You have to find the people to do the work associated with the project; they are also often part-time because they have other operational responsibilities. Being faced with the prospect of managing a project forces you to ask if you have all the skills necessary. Help is at hand – that is the purpose of this book. It is designed to give you some guidance through the process of managing a project effectively and to become better at the job.

The book is written to give you practical and well-tested techniques to improve your performance and meet your needs if you:

❑ have just been given a project to manage;
❑ have managed projects before but seek to improve your skills;
❑ are a team member and want to learn project skills.

The processes, procedures and techniques used by project managers are not difficult to learn. Application is not always easy due to the complexity of the work. Success does depend on your taking a disciplined approach to create new working habits. This is your first step in the change process: existing habits are in our comfort zone. To adopt new habits is a painful process, rather like a new pair of shoes – they are uncomfortable for the first few days until we wear them in!

But the little pain caused is worth tolerating for the significant benefits that you will gain from recognition by others that you are a proficient project manager.

Steps to Improve

1. Recognize that you face change in your life continually.
2. Accept that change is an inevitability of development and growth.
3. Regard change as a challenge to help you improve things.
4. Determine to learn the skills of managing the change process.

WHY ARE PROJECTS SPECIAL?

Projects at work involve the processes we use to create something we currently do not have, but desire as a matter of strategic need. Any project is an activity beyond what we can regard as the routine business activity of the organization. This sets the project apart as something that must receive special treatment.

QUESTION 1

Identify three of the projects you know have been active in your organization in the past few months. Write down what is special about these activities that makes them different from everyday routine work.

Perhaps you have written down a number of particular characteristics of these activities called 'projects'. Have you concluded that projects nearly always have one common attribute? The project is an additional set of activities on top of your normal operational duties that you are expected to carry out as part of your job. This has a tendency to create an overload condition leading to increased stress. It makes prioritizing the day's work more difficult as we react to the fire-fighting situations that always seem to invade our attempts to maintain an orderly diary!

It is only the very large projects that have full-time dedicated teams, released from any other duties for the life of the project. The project has significant benefits which are often ignored:

❑ a unique opportunity to learn new skills and technology;
❑ a valuable way to improve the performance of everyone involved;
❑ an opportunity to create new and more effective working practices.

This leads us to a definition for a project:

DEFINITION – A PROJECT IS. . .

a collection of linked activities, carried out in an organized manner, with a clearly defined
                    START POINT and END POINT
to achieve some specific results desired to satisfy the strategic needs of the organization at the current time.

As it is a special activity you will need to use a different approach to achieve the results. You are in a temporary management role as the project manager, faced with the difficult task of managing a small team of people drawn from different departments.

There is a strong possibility that the team membership will change with time as the priorities in the participating departments change from week to week. This flexibility has some potential advantages, but usually imposes additional focus on the need for effective communication, negotiation and influencing skills to maintain control of the project.

WHAT ARE THE SKILLS YOU WILL NEED?

Of course it is expected you have the skills required to apply the techniques for effective management of a project. One purpose of this book is to help you with these techniques. You will also need to stretch your knowledge and skills in many other ways:

- ❑ to set targets for people which are aligned to their personal goals;
- ❑ create a strong sense of responsibility for the project work;
- ❑ create commitment in the team members;
- ❑ coach the team members in many aspects of the work;
- ❑ learn from experts to increase your own knowledge;
- ❑ explain your and management decisions;
- ❑ encourage people to maintain interest and motivation;
- ❑ regularly keep everyone informed of progress;
- ❑ promote an atmosphere supporting free and willing feedback;
- ❑ manage peer and senior groups to influence their support;
- ❑ manage third parties such as contractors and consultants;
- ❑ manage conflict in the team;
- ❑ help the team members to prioritize their workloads;
- ❑ show your concern for continuous improvement;
- ❑ take risks and short cuts in the interests of the project.

Your team will expect you to champion their interests at all times to keep them enthusiastic about the project. At the same time you must ensure you understand where the project fits in to the organizational strategy. The prospect may be daunting, even enough to put you off project work altogether! Regard it as a real challenge to learn and improve as you become an even better project manager.

WHAT IS PROJECT MANAGEMENT?

Project management has traditionally been seen as comprising the skills you need to effectively manage a project. As we have discussed, a project is a way to create change, to provide us with something we don't have at present. Change is not static, it is a dynamic process, continually moving, we hope in one direction, under a set of conditions which we attempt to control. So project management must be a dynamic process, embracing the techniques we use with the people to achieve the desired results. A typical definition is:

DEFINITION – PROJECT MANAGEMENT IS. . .

the dynamic process that utilizes the appropriate resources of the organization in a controlled and structured manner, to achieve some clearly defined objectives identified as strategic needs.
It is always conducted within a defined set of constraints.

As a process it is characterized by being:

❏ objectives-oriented – otherwise why do it?
❏ change-oriented – to create something you need;
❏ multi-disciplined – using many skills to achieve success;
❏ opportunistic – bypassing the old norms and seeking new ideas;
❏ control-oriented – without which you may never finish;
❏ performance-oriented – setting high standards of work and quality;
❏ questioning – throwing off old traditions and habits to expose the new.

In the majority of organizations the role of project manager is a temporary management activity associated only with a specific project – although it is possible you have more than one active at the same time!

This makes the job more complex than that of a manager of a section or department in a fixed hierarchy. You will need the same skills as your colleagues in such a role, with the added complexity of:

❏ managing team members drawn from different departments, who have their own responsibilities outside the project work;
❏ the risk of instability in the team due to changing priorities of the line managers of your team members;

❑ creating an effective team environment with a changing team;
❑ building a team quickly with people who do not know each other;
❑ poor communication and sharing of information because the team members do not know or necessarily trust each other;
❑ focusing the team members on performance which may not be consistent with their personal goals agreed with their line manager;
❑ creating a team 'identity' to encourage the team members to meet regularly and learn more about each other and promote good team-working.

The organizational structure provides the matrix from which your team is drawn. During the early part of the project, everyone is getting used to working in a new environment with different colleagues. This can lead to some conflict as the team learns to work together and establish the team norms and behaviours. Success does not come as a result of just using the right tools and techniques. It is achieved by using your skills as a leader to manage the team effectively and overcome the areas of potential difficulty to reduce the risk of failure.

QUESTION 2

What else do you think you can do with the team members to ensure that these difficulties are minimized and kept within your control, particularly during the early stages of the project?

Although you know you must do everything you think necessary to make the project a success, do not expect a quiet life! You expect to always get full cooperation, enthusiastic support, strong commitment and willing guidance and advice, but projects are often the target of open opposition, political manoeuvring, subtle interference, conflict and even sabotage!

YOUR ROLE AS THE PROJECT MANAGER

You have to devote your efforts to maintaining a balance between the demands and needs of:

❑ the customer;
❑ the project;
❑ the project team; and
❑ the organization.

These demands provide a real challenge to manage your time effectively, to prioritize your efforts, and to influence your team to do the same. Good control of the work sustains the momentum of the project while allowing non-project activities to continue to be completed as required. As the project manager you are:

❑ expected to demonstrate proven skills in the use of project tools and techniques;
❑ expected to demonstrate effective team leadership skills;
❑ limited in authority to secure resources;
❑ forced to work across departmental boundaries;
❑ expected to conform to established working practices;
❑ working with the unknown and unpredictable;
❑ expected to maintain control in a situation subject to risks;
❑ expected to maintain an agreed schedule in spite of issues arising.

You are expected to accept *responsibility* for the project and report the progress regularly to senior management. It is an accepted concept that this reporting channel should focus on just one senior manager of your organization. We will call this person the *project sponsor* who is *accountable* for the project success. This should ensure that there is continuing support and commitment from the organization for the project work. The sponsor must ensure that the project direction is aligned to

strategic objectives and communicate the priority and importance of the project to everyone who has an interest in it. The
sponsor is a major *stakeholder* in the project, along with the
customer who wants the results.

DEFINITION
– A PROJECT STAKEHOLDER IS . . .

any person, group of people or organization who has a vested
interest in the project now or in the future. Some are more
important than others to support your efforts.
The interest may be positive: supporting a successful outcome, or
negative: striving to hinder or stop the project!

You must manage the stakeholders to achieve a successful result
and, as we will see later, they have a direct impact on the
project. As the project manager you must:

- ❑ select your core team – the team members who will stay
  with the project;
- ❑ identify and manage the stakeholders;
- ❑ define the project objectives, deliverables and scope;
- ❑ manage the project risks;
- ❑ plan the project and derive an acceptable schedule for the
  work;
- ❑ allocate responsibilities for the work;
- ❑ secure resource commitments;
- ❑ monitor and track progress;
- ❑ resolve the problems that occur;
- ❑ control the project costs;
- ❑ report the progress to the major or *key stakeholders*.

We are using some common management language here:

QUESTION 3

What do you understand by the terms:

Responsibility   *Authority*   *Accountability?*

Write down your definition for these three terms when applied to a project.

Steps to Improve

1. Ensure you know who is sponsoring your project.
2. Clarify what is expected of you as the project manager.
3. Check your understanding of what the role involves with the sponsor.

ANSWERS

Question 1
Most projects can be characterized as:

- ❏ having a specific and defined purpose;
- ❏ unique because it will never be repeated in quite the same way;
- ❏ being focused on customer needs and expectations;
- ❏ not being routine but including many routine-type tasks;
- ❏ having defined constraints of time, cost and people available;
- ❏ involving people in different departments and even sites;
- ❏ involving many unknowns and hence many risks;
- ❏ challenging traditional ways of working to introduce improvements;
- ❏ providing an opportunity to learn new skills.

Question 2
You need to understand your team members and this only comes from regular contact to build a relationship with each. Establish a practice from the outset of having regular one-to-one semi-formal discussions to learn about their interests, experience, skills and concerns about their work. This aids team-working and develops a mutual trust and respect between you and your team, encouraging open sharing and feedback.

Question 3
Compare your definitions with these:
Responsibility is the obligation to ensure all the project tasks allocated to an individual are carried out on time to the appropriate standards. Responsibility must be clearly defined and cannot be shared – a split responsibility soon becomes no responsibility with no ownership accepted by any individual.
Authority is the right to take and implement decisions about people, equipment, materials and money. Authority must be clearly defined, preferably in writing and specific to the project.
Accountability is the management control over authority given by delegation. No authority means no accountability for management decisions. Accountability is often confused with responsibility when used to emphasize importance or priority of a task.

3

THE PROJECT MANAGER AND LEADERSHIP

Your ability to lead a team will be tested to the full as you strive to achieve success in your project. You are working with and through others, using these skills to energize and direct a diverse group of people to give a high performance, willingly and enthusiastically throughout the project. These people come from different parts of the organization, where every department has its own culture through the leadership style of the departmental manager. You have to work with these cultural variations to create a climate of cooperation and coordinate the efforts of the team members without having direct line authority.

Ask some of your colleagues who have managed projects in your organization which of the following characteristics are desirable:

❑ flexible and adaptable to changing requirements;
❑ able to use initiative;
❑ assertive and confident;
❑ ambitious with plenty of drive, energy and commitment;
❑ an effective communicator and good listener;
❑ enthusiastic about the project and creative;
❑ well organized and self-disciplined in managing time;
❑ a generalist rather then a specialist – having technical awareness;
❑ able to facilitate problem solving with the team;

❑ able to make and take decisions without procrastinating;
❑ promote a motivating climate in the team;
❑ focused on the project objectives, to maintain other's focus;
❑ trained in project techniques and having practical experience of their use.

The autocratic leader tends to tell people what to do, using a 'you will' approach. The other extreme, the democratic leader, encourages open sharing of information, consulting widely and asking people to do the work using a 'will you (please)' approach. The latter style at times appears as though a favour is being requested rather than responsibility being clearly allocated. In practice most managers adopt a style, like a mask, that is often dictated by:

❑ the situation and the prevailing environment;
❑ the type of work, its priority and urgency;
❑ the way the team members react and behave in the environment.

When a crisis hits, some managers adopt a more autocratic style in the interest of getting a quick result. It is perceived that no time exists for consultation; ideas and suggestions are not encouraged and consensus is avoided. The actions required are dictated by command and control. The democratic style is regarded as slower, encouraging people to give their ideas and opinions, always seeking a consensus so the team is fully involved and well motivated to achieve results. But there is often a time penalty for these processes which is not always compatible with the demands of a time-limited project.

What is appropriate for your role as project manager? There is no 'right' style – only a style that seems to work with the people at the time. You must learn to recognize what approach is appropriate at any particular time to get results in the specialized situation of a project because of:

❑ the nature of the work, which is time and cost constrained;

❏ the diverse range of skills and experience of people you do not know well during the early stages.

You must make things happen and this is only achieved through a sustained focus on three important areas:

1. Ensuring all the project tasks are clearly defined and completed on time to the desired quality.
2. Ensuring the work is well coordinated and fairly distributed in the team to encourage effective teamworking.
3. Ensuring the individual team members understand their role and responsibilities and are given guidance and opportunity to develop their skills.

All are directed to achieving the project objectives and deliverables that will eventually provide the benefits expected by your customer (see Figure 3.1). You must try and keep a balance between these three areas, giving an appropriate time to each. If you get too involved with any one, the other two will tend to

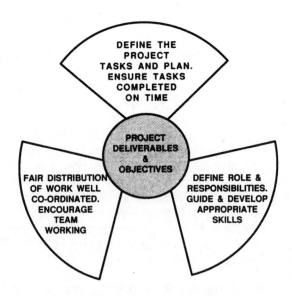

Figure 3.1 *Project deliverables and objectives*

suffer from your lack of attention. If you give yourself a large amount of the project work, you will find it difficult to give time to support and guide individual team members or focus on the project tasks and plan.

If you hit a significant problem you move into a crisis mode. Once some actions are agreed to resolve the problem, it is easy to adopt an autocratic style to get the action list tasks done as soon as possible. This task orientation is potentially dangerous if you allow it to continue after the crisis is resolved, as the team will perceive you are not interested in teamwork or individual people. Always remember to take a step away from the current situation and take an overview or balanced view again. This keeps the three areas in focus and all directed in one fundamental direction – the project objectives.

The actions you take at each stage of the project are focused on maintaining this balance, adopting a range of styles according to the prevailing situation. However, in any project the people involved are not just yourself and the team. Earlier in this chapter we identified the people or groups referred to as the *stakeholders*. You have a *customer* – the person or group of people who expect to receive the outcomes, and a *project sponsor* who is accountable for the project results. There are also many others who have an interest in what you are going to do in your project.

THE PROJECT STAKEHOLDERS

Anyone in the organization who potentially at some time has an interest in your project is a stakeholder. You need to identify these people because they are certain to attempt to exert influence on how you manage the project. The team members come from different departments and their line managers have agreed to losing their resource for some of the working weeks ahead. The line managers are often *key stakeholders* – they can have a significant impact on your project if their priorities change and you lose a promised resource.

QUESTION 4

Identify a project in which you have been involved. Who were the people or groups who had an interest and made up the stakeholder group? Write down as many as you can remember. Were they all known at the outset or did some appear to demonstrate interest later?

All stakeholders have a hidden agenda about what they expect from your project, particularly those inside your organization. You need to expose these expectations before you define the project. This is not always easy where there is a political dimension to stakeholder needs and expectations – one need could be to hinder or stop the project!

Stakeholders are not only inside the organization: many external people are expecting to have work from your project – suppliers, contractors, consultants and possibly government departments or agencies. All have their reasons for becoming involved in the project. You have little or no authority over any of your stakeholders and it is a formidable challenge to manage them effectively and retain their help and support throughout the project.

Steps to Improve

1. Recognize that you need leadership skills as a project manager.
2. If appropriate, seek leadership skills training.
3. Accept that you must lead a project team; you cannot control it.
4. Remember to step away from detail for the overview of what is happening.
5. Seek advice and support from colleagues and others.

ANSWERS

Question 4
The more common stakeholders in a project may include:

The sponsor (as representative of the senior management)
The customer
The end user
The project manager
The project team
The line managers of the team members
The finance department (representative)
The sales department (representative)
The marketing department (representative)
The technical department
Documentation and records department
The information services department
The service department (representative)
Other departments
Consultants – various
Sub-contractors – various
Suppliers – various at different times
Other agencies
Other divisions
Clients of the customer
The public (or representative body).

4

THE DIMENSIONS OF PROJECT LEADERSHIP

You can now see that your role of project manager is complex, leading a team and a diverse group of other people to achieve the project objectives. The stakeholders can have a significant impact on your success through their direct or indirect influence on each of the areas you are managing to achieve the project objectives as seen in Figure 4.1. You spend much of your time inner-directed, focusing on the project tasks, developing and maintaining good teamwork and making sure you have the right skills in the team. You are also outer-directed, spending time with your stakeholders to understand their needs and expectations, use their skills when appropriate and keep them informed of progress.

You cannot ignore your stakeholders, you must manage them. They can influence your project at any time with serious consequences to progress. This leads us to the first dimension of project leadership:

Identify and manage the project stakeholders.

There is often a misunderstanding about where to start a project. When everyone involved is enthusiastic about the project there is a driving need to get going, and this can lead to a disorganized and unstructured approach to the work. To avoid any confusion, think of all projects as following a simple life-cycle of four phases:

❑ definition of the project objectives;

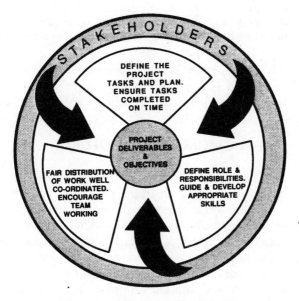

Figure 4.1 *Impact of stakeholders*

❏ planning the project work;
❏ executing the project work;
❏ closing the project and hand over to the customer.

In practice these are not discrete sequential phases because you may have to redefine or replan at any time through the project. The phases are a convenient way to introduce some discipline into the project process and ensure certain checks are carried out at appropriate points. All the phases are dynamic and subject to review and revision at any time after the start-up of the project. This gives us the second dimension of project leadership:

Manage (ie, control) the project dynamic life-cycle from definition through planning and execution to closure – all the tasks of the project.

The third dimension of project leadership is more closely focused on the three areas where you spend the majority of your time, to manage the performance of everyone involved:

Manage the performance of yourself, the team and the stake-holders to ensure high standards and quality are sustained at all times.

Success with your project is directly related to balancing the time and effort you give to each of these dimensions from the start-up until you hand over the results to your customer.

MANAGING STAKEHOLDERS

Identifying stakeholders is not just part of the project start-up. Many do not appear until later in the project so you must keep a look out for new ones appearing – usually when you least expect them! The relative importance of each changes with time and the stages of the project. If you fail to recognize or cooperate with any stakeholder you take a serious risk. That stakeholder could force views or changes to your plans at a time that is least convenient to you and hinder progress. You are the project manager and must set the ground rules from the outset.

It may be helpful to identify stakeholders as having different levels of importance for your project. The sponsor and customer are clearly of *high* importance, but others could be ranked *medium* or *low* importance.

Ask your sponsor to inform all your internal (your organization's) stakeholders about the strategic importance and priority of your project. This makes your job easier when you approach them later for active support of your efforts. Many of the stakeholders have valuable knowledge and experience. If appropriate, use this experience for your project and seek their input when you feel it can help the team. You can even bring a stakeholder into the team for a time if he or she can make a specific contribution.

You must sustain stakeholder support and commitment, so part of your tactics is to encourage that support as diplomatically as possible. You are the project manager, so make sure they:

❑ understand your responsibilities and authority;
❑ accept you are in charge of the daily work of the team;

❏ are encouraged to make positive suggestions;
❏ can contribute their ideas.

React promptly to covert criticism or interference that demotivates the team, destroys team spirit and promotes conflict. Poor stakeholder control can lead to chaos, confusion and demotivation of your team through their perceived interference. With your team ask:

❏ Who are the stakeholders?
❏ Which are internal and external to the organization?
❏ What needs to be known about each stakeholder?
❏ Where and how can this information be gathered?

Then gather information about each:

❏ What exactly is the interest?
❏ Why are they interested?
❏ What are they expecting to gain?
❏ How will the project affect them?
❏ Can they contribute experience or knowledge?
❏ Are there hidden agendas and if so, what are they?
❏ What authority does the stakeholder have?
❏ Are there likely to be contractual implications?
❏ Are they in favour of the project?
❏ Will the project interfere with their operations?
❏ Could they seriously hinder or block the project progress?

The list of stakeholders will change or grow with time, so draw up a list at the beginning of the project, recording the stakeholder's name, location, address if appropriate, and contact telephone number.

It is important to recognize this is not a static list: it does change. Review your list of stakeholders at regular intervals and keep the record up to date. Distribute the list to all stakeholders to show you recognize their interest. Meet with them regularly to understand changes in their needs. Keep them informed of progress.

MANAGING THE PROJECT DYNAMIC LIFE-CYCLE

This involves you in:

❑ defining the project deliverables;
❑ controlling the project tasks;
❑ securing the resources needed to complete the tasks on time;
❑ procuring all the materials and equipment required;
❑ controlling the project work to stay on track to a schedule;
❑ dealing with changes;
❑ managing project risks;
❑ resolving issues that arise;
❑ demonstrating your concern for your team members;
❑ controlling sub-contractors and suppliers;
❑ handing over the results to your customer on time.

The team are looking to you as their leader to provide them with a congenial working environment and to give support and guidance. Chapters 6–14 take you through the life-cycle process and the actions you take as the project manager to achieve a successful outcome from your project.

MANAGING PERFORMANCE

As the project manager you must demonstrate your concern about the performance of everyone involved with the work of the project.

You are responsible for delivering the results expected by the *key stakeholders*, so start with yourself. Evaluate your perform-ance regularly to help you improve the way you do the job. Spend a few minutes at the end of each day to ask:

❑ What should I have achieved today?
    – What have I achieved today?
    – What have I done well?
    – What could I have done better?
    – What must I do to follow-up?

❏ What issues remain unresolved?
   – What issues need to be discussed with my sponsor?
   – What is their urgency?
❏ What decisions did I take today?
   – On reflection, were they the right decisions?
   – Did I consult the right people before the decision?
   – When should I review and evaluate the decisions taken?
❏ What problems surfaced with the team members?
   – Did I deal with these fairly?
   – What decisions have I put off?
   ·– When must I deal with these decisions?
❏ Did I have contact with the team members today?
   – Is everyone aware of progress?
   – Are communication processes working well?
   – Do I need to reinforce or modify communication
     methods?
   – Is teamworking effective?
   – What can I do to improve teamwork?
   – Do I need to do anything to improve performance?
   – Did I miss an opportunity to coach someone today?
❏ What actions must I take tomorrow?

Prepare an action list before leaving the office, then review it the next morning before implementing the actions. Remember to set up diary dates for one-to-one discussions with your sponsor and each team member. These help you build the working relationships you need to monitor and aid performance in the interests of the project. You might feel these discussions are not necessary with people you believe you know well. However well you think you know someone, you must still have these dialogues to talk about:

❏ performance issues;
❏ how they feel about your leadership and their work;
❏ what they hope to gain from the project;
❏ their personal objectives.

The stakeholders provide the drive, direction and climate for success. Ignore them and you court potential disaster! Pay particular attention to:

❏ keeping key stakeholders regularly informed of progress;
❏ reminding them of their commitments of support;
❏ involving appropriate stakeholders in important decisions;
❏ involving them in replanning or solving problems;
❏ monitoring team members responsible for other stake-holders;
❏ encouraging the team to maintain good communications with stakeholders.

WHAT ABOUT TEAMWORK?

Because most projects involve more than one person, teamwork is crucial to achieve success. You are starting a project by taking a group of people, possibly from different backgrounds, with different experience, skills and personal needs to build them into a cohesive working unit. Unless you have a dedicated team with full-time members, the team members are only giving part of their working day or week to your project activities. Each then has a divided loyalty to their line manager and the project which may require different working practices. The complexity increases if they are working in more than one project team at the same time.

The first time you bring your core team together they are really a group of individuals. They may not have worked with each other before even if they know one another. They come from different functions and their behaviour at work is con-ditioned by their normal operational environment. You are an unknown entity to them with your own style to which they must quickly become accustomed.

They expect you to start to build the group into a team. Have a clear sense of direction to make this complex process a little easier. Everyone should know that they are in the team because all have experience and skills you consider relevant to the project. Your objective is to harness their abilities, creativity and efforts to achieve a shared goal or outcome.

You are embarking on a journey to create something new so it is an exciting place to work and you want creative, enthusiastic people with a strong sense of responsibility and commitment. A successful team consists of a carefully designed mixture of the right skills and personalities who can work together without dissension and conflict.

˙ A balanced team, encouraged to mature its working norms quickly, can manage overwhelming difficulties and achieve what appears at times to be a 'mission impossible'.

Steps to Improve

1. Recognize the impact of the three dimensions on project success.
2. Develop your skills to manage performance.
3. Identify all your project stakeholders and get to know them.
4. Set up regular one-to-ones with the team and stakeholders.
5. Allow time to reflect and examine your own performance.
6. Create a climate which encourages effective teamwork.

A CASE STUDY

We are now introducing you to a case study that continues through the remainder of this work. The purpose is to expose some of the typical situations that you will certainly meet in your project work and then examine how you would react in your organization. Of course the culture of your organization will influence you as there is never an absolutely right or wrong answer. It allows us to examine how you can improve your management of the team in a project situation.

The first step is to carefully read the brief and the details about your team. As you read on you will find many scenarios where you are asked to take a decision about what you will do faced with a particular situation. Decide which of the two, three or more optional actions you would select and why. When considering these scenarios remember to note down the assumptions you make. Some suggested responses are given in Appendix 1.

CASE STUDY

You have just been informed of your appointment to lead a new project approved by the Projects Steering Group. Your director has been appointed as the project sponsor and you are told that you must be prepared to give 50 per cent of your time to the project and assign some of your current responsibilities to other members of your departmental team. The initial proposal document you are given was prepared by someone else some three months earlier and this divided the project into some discrete parts:

- ❑ data gathering
- ❑ development
- ❑ prototype testing
- ❑ final testing
- ❑ implementation and training
- ❑ support and maintenance services.

The budget approved for the project is based on a core team of six people with additional team support as required during the project life. However, your sponsor informs you that even though this is regarded by the organization as an important high profile project, only five people can be spared at the current time due to workload. All the core team member allocations have been agreed with their line managers.

The project is important and the deliverables listed in the original proposal are regarded as still valid and essential to the organization. The 'business critical date' for the project has been fixed by its interface with another project currently active at another location. This date effectively gives you exactly 58 calendar weeks from now to complete the project. It has been made very clear that the directors regard this project as having a 'MUST NOT FAIL' label and that no slippages will be tolerated.

Only one of the team members is known to you, having worked with you before in the same team on a previous project. One member of the team has been assigned at your request. As you have little information on the other team members you call the Personnel Manager and ask for a brief note of their backgrounds with particular reference to project work. The response you receive gives you only some basic information.

YOUR TEAM

Graham

A very experienced person with over 15 years with the organization. He worked with you previously on the DAMOS project and you value his knowledge and project skills. You feel fortunate to have him assigned full time on the project although you know he is regarded as being difficult sometimes. He has a reputation for being dogmatic and scornful of others' ability in comparison to his long experience. This makes him a little cynical about some modern technology and ideas that he has not generated. Apparently, for the next four weeks he has a little 'tidying-up' to do on the last project.

Alison

An experienced person with some specific skills needed on this project. Her release for this project is full time but apparently this has been imposed on her line manager who is not happy about the situation. You expect this to lead to some conflict problems about work prioritization as her line manager continues to try and assign her work. She has been with the organization since leaving university and although she has worked in various departments during the past ten years, there has been no significant increase in her responsibilities. She is a popular person and very participative in the social activities in the organization.

Ian

You asked for Ian, knowing he has a detailed knowledge and interest in the project. He is a quiet, academic type with an analytical approach which you feel will be valuable to the work ahead. Like many academic types he often gives the appearance of being quite disorganized. Ian will give 60 per cent of his time to the project and, having two people reporting to him, can easily pull in additional resource support.

Dave

He is a young business graduate almost at the end of his first year with the organization. His manager requested his assignment to the project as an opportunity to experence project work under your guidance. What he lacks in experience is made up for by his enthusiasm and keenness to learn. He will be full time on the project.

Janet

Janet is a very competent analyst who joined the organization from a competitor almost two years ago, bringing with her a good knowledge of the market place. Her marketing experience has quickly gained her a reputation in the organization and her opinions are highly regarded by the directors. She has a strong commitment to her work and is intolerant of poor quality work and incompetence. She will be assigned 70 per cent of her time to the project, but must give time to her work associated with another project launching a new product.

After some discussions with your sponsor you accept who is to join the project team and you review the information you gather about each. You then decide the first step is to get the team together, so you prepare a short memo asking them to attend an initial kick-off meeting five days from now. Having issued the memo you organize a meeting room and start thinking about how you will conduct this meeting.

CASE STUDY – SCENARIO I

The day of your first team meeting has arrived and is due to start in half an hour. Everyone has confirmed their attendance. They have no details of the project except they have been told the project assignment will be for 12 months. Your sponsor has also confirmed he will be present. A good strategy for this kick-off meeting is:

1. Explain the project overall objectives and ask them for their ideas and suggestions to identify how to approach the project.
   OR
2. Ask the sponsor to introduce the project and emphasize the project context and importance to the organization. Then introduce your thoughts on the processes to follow for the project
   OR
3. Explain the technical details of the project and what is expected by the organization. Focus the team to discuss how these can be achieved.

6

PROJECT START-UP

Call a kick-off meeting with the sponsor and team, to ensure you have a clear understanding of the project purpose and how it aligns to the strategic needs of the organization. The project start-up is often confused and 'fuzzy' because you may have:

- ❏ unclear direction;
- ❏ uncertainties about what is really required by everyone interested in the outcomes;
- ❏ confusion because people can not stand back and take a holistic view;
- ❏ unknowns about how to get some results;
- ❏ no clear idea of benefits which can be defined;
- ❏ no clear information on resources available;
- ❏ no clear idea about how long it will take.

Although you and your team are enthusiastic and keen to get going, it is prudent to review just what information you can now assemble to ensure the project does not set off in the wrong direction. If you do not have this data, assign tasks in the team to collect it as soon as possible. Ask some fundamental questions.

WHO IS THE REAL CUSTOMER?

Ensure you are clear:

- ❏ who your customer is;

❏ who your main contact is since you must start to build a working relationship with this individual – the *customer representative*.

If there are multiple customers, even inside the organization, each will have their own personal perceptions of what they want from your project and these perceptions will frequently generate hostility and conflict.

Action Point

Identify and understand the needs and expectations of each customer

The customer representative is the key individual (preferably not a committee) who has the necessary authority to take decisions affecting the project. For some larger strategic projects your organization may prefer to appoint a *project board*. This ensures that the departments which will be affected by the project and its outcomes are all represented as a collective customer. The chairperson of the project board is given the authority to act on behalf of the board when necessary.

WHO ARE THE END-USERS?

The customer wants the results from the project, but the *end-users* are the group of people who will actually use the results on a day-to-day basis. You need to have contact with the end-users or a representative of this group to check that you understand their needs and concerns about how the results will be used. You may decide to include this person in your project team. On larger projects a *user group* is sometimes appointed.

HOW IS THE CUSTOMER SATISFIED?

Recognize that customer expectations directly relate to customer satisfaction. Unfortunately there are degrees of satisfaction relating to the extent to which your customer perceives you understand their expectations and, what is more important, meet them with the results achieved. Fall short of these expectations and you have an unhappy rather than a delighted customer. Fall short on the quality or performance standards expected and you will create a complaining customer, particularly if you:

❑ do not deliver on time – to the agreed schedule of delivery;
❑ increase the project cost.

You risk losing the respect of the customer and there is the further problem of recovering the additional cost from a disgruntled customer. Customers also expect you and your project team:

❑ to serve them with professional competence;
❑ to behave in a cooperative and friendly manner;
❑ to understand their environment;
❑ to understand the difficulties and constraints they face;
❑ not to add to their problems;
❑ to avoid springing surprises;
❑ to provide positive results, not excuses for poor performance.

WHAT ARE THE CUSTOMER NEEDS?

Understanding the needs of the customer allows you to produce a project definition to meet the customer's expectations. These are the customer requirements that drive the planning process. This is the solid foundation for your project. Failure to give this activity appropriate time and effort will have continual impact on the project throughout its life. Ask questions to:

❑ understand your customer;

❑ understand the customer's environment;
❑ use political skills – not all customers are equal and some needs cannot be addressed for political reasons;
❑ demonstrate your awareness of their technical needs;
❑ ensure customer and end-user needs are aligned;
❑ analyse the mixed signals you receive through personal influences on needs;
❑ expose any hidden expectations.

The data you and your team gather at this stage provide the inputs for the project definition. Beware the potential traps:

❑ avoid seeking technical perfection beyond current capability or known state-of-the-art – simplicity is often more effective;
❑ confirm that the customer understands the risks of going for leading-edge solutions;
❑ watch out for bias filters – it is easy for you to dismiss needs for which you cannot think of an easy solution because it is outside your experience or knowledge.

Deriving the statement of needs is a partnership between you and your customer. Working with your customers can be frustrating. At times you will need to exercise all your communication skills to achieve an open relationship. This places an obligation on your customer to enter into the partnership with a serious intent to contribute openly and not to sit on hidden agendas.

Try to persuade your customer to adopt a total life-cycle approach for the project, starting with needs and requirements through planning, execution, hand over and full implementation. This helps the customer to focus on the need for you to:

❑ derive an acceptance process for hand over;
❑ define follow-on activities – service, support, etc.

WHAT ARE THE PROJECT CONSTRAINTS?

The constraints limit all project activities throughout the project life-cycle. It is unlikely you will have unlimited resources, funding and time to complete the work. The project may yield significantly reduced benefits if you provide the results late – the requirements or the market needs may have changed dramatically!

If you are intending to develop a new product, the date of availability to the sales team is critical to acquiring a significant market share and beating the competition. If the sales team cannot satisfy their customers and break promises, they risk losing important accounts. The organization's credibility and reputation will suffer. It is always difficult to convince a frustrated customer such things will not happen again. Business needs are continually changing. Even with an internal project, late completion may lead others to conclude the whole effort was a waste of time, because of new requirements. Project 'drift' sets in and you acquire a legacy of the 'project manager with the endless project'.

Ensure as early as possible that all known constraints are identified. They usually fall into three categories:

❑ *financial* – project cost, capital costs, materials, revenue and resource costs;
❑ *time* – time to deliver the results, the critical date when the results are needed;
❑ *quality* – the scope, specifications and standards to be achieved.

Explore each with your customer to gather the information needed to guarantee success.

WHAT DOCUMENTATION IS REQUIRED?

Project work produces a large amount of data and it is important that you record essential material. Start off your project by avoiding the 'I'll do it my way' syndrome.

Insist that the team keep all essential project records on standard forms designed to record the data you need for good control. Throughout this book at the appropriate time, we will identify such requirements. This ensures everyone involved

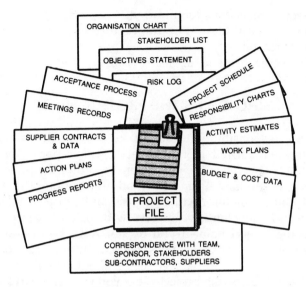

Figure 6.1 *Project file*

with the project records data in a consistent and disciplined manner without re-inventing forms every week. In addition you get the right information recorded (and in the appropriate volume) for the project file to support your control system and aid project evaluation at completion.

Expect an adverse reaction from people - it is viewed as 'form-filling' and a chore. Stress the importance of keeping everyone informed about what has happened in the project and that it is in their interests to get into the habit of keeping accurate records. Nobody can carry all the plans and information in their head! All the templates suggested in Figure 6.1 can be designed on a computer and networked for ease of completion from blank masters.

All these forms will carry some common essential information:

❏ project title or name – use a short acronym for identity;
❏ project sponsor's name;
❏ project manager's name;

❑ project number for identification;
❑ security classification if appropriate;
❑ date prepared;
❑ date of current issue, ie, last revision.

WHO OWNS THE PROJECT FILE?

It is your responsibility to set up a project file for all the documentation related to the project – either paper- or computer-based. This file is the permanent record of the project and requires a disciplined approach to administration. This makes the distribution of information, access and retrieval relatively easy. There is a potential difficulty with using a computer to store all the project data. If you do not restrict access to your data, people can make changes without informing you and create confusion. If you have concerns about reliability, always keep a hard copy of the project file – you cannot always take a computer into meetings off-site!

Organize your project file into sections for the different stages of the project, for example:

❑ background information;
❑ project definition;
❑ project plans and schedules;
❑ project execution and implementation;
❑ project closure.

Divide into more detail if necessary. You are responsible for updating the file at regular intervals and it is a good habit to do this once a week. Always let others know where to find the file – it is most frustrating to search for a file that is hidden away!

WHY USE A PROJECT LOG BOOK?

It is a good discipline to open a project log book at the start of your project, as shown in Figure 6.2. This records all events, agreed actions and forward planning ideas. The book is an A4 bound, lined book and *not* a loose-leaf file or folder.

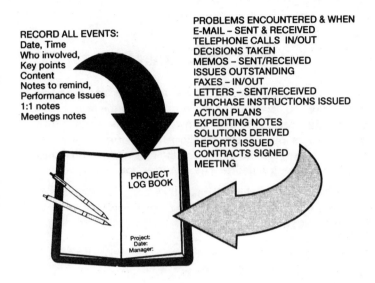

RECORD ALL EVENTS:
Date, Time
Who involved,
Key points
Content
Notes to remind,
Performance Issues
1:1 notes
Meetings notes

PROBLEMS ENCOUNTERED & WHEN
E-MAIL – SENT & RECEIVED
TELEPHONE CALLS IN/OUT
DECISIONS TAKEN
MEMOS – SENT/RECEIVED
ISSUES OUTSTANDING
FAXES – IN/OUT
LETTERS – SENT/RECEIVED
PURCHASE INSTRUCTIONS ISSUED
ACTION PLANS
EXPEDITING NOTES
SOLUTIONS DERIVED
REPORTS ISSUED
CONTRACTS SIGNED
MEETING

PROJECT
LOG BOOK

Project:
Date:
Manager:

Figure 6.2 *Project log book*

The log book is *not* a personal document – it is an addendum to the project file. When using a log book:

❏ use every page and number them sequentially;
❏ *never* remove any pages;
❏ start each day with a new page;
❏ *always* write in pen, ball-point or felt tip, *never* pencil;
❏ write on every line;
❏ rule out all unused lines at the end of each day and sign the page at the bottom;
❏ do not allow anyone else to write in the log book – not even the project sponsor.

The log book is particularly valuable to record events with third parties like suppliers and contractors. When conflict and differences occur the log book provides a record of events that often takes the heat out of an argument. The record can have a legal status if a dispute eventually ends up in the hands of the lawyers.

CASE STUDY – SCENARIO 2

At your project kick-off meetings your sponsor has described the organization's expectations of the work you and the team must carry out. In the discussion that follows the team identify that the deliverables of the project for the named customer will be very similar to those required by another internal customer. Although the project has been initiated by one customer you should:

1. Decide to ignore this information as it is only based on rumour and is not a formal request for a project. Focus the team on the known customer
    OR
2. Assign tasks to the team to determine unofficially if a competitive project is about to start
    OR
3. Tell the team you will send a memo to all divisional managers informing them about this project and ask them directly about their possible future interest
    OR
    Is there another option you would take?

Steps to Improve

1. Focus the team on identifying all the customer needs.
2. Understand your customer's business operations.
3. Ask searching questions to confirm all the project constraints.
4. Organize your project documentation to record essential facts.
5. Explain to the team why accurate records are important to the project.
6. Start a project log book now.

7

DEFINING YOUR PROJECT

You may ask at this point, 'What is the difference between start-up and definition?' The first is a data-gathering activity. Definition is the process of turning the data into something that is no longer just a wish or a hope. You have spent a considerable amount of time and effort to gather all the relevant data in the start-up process to design the foundations of your project. This project definition is supported by numerous documents as appropriate to the project.

Failure to give adequate time to this activity and derive all the relevant data for these foundations leads to a poorly defined project with a considerably reduced chance of achieving a successful outcome.

WHAT IS NECESSARY TO DEFINE A PROJECT?

This definition phase is where many projects go wrong – often because there is no clear definition or it has remained confused with so many different stakeholder inputs. Remember, successful definition must involve all the team at every step, to build their acceptance and commitment to the work of the project.

QUESTION 5

What do you need to write down now to define your project? List what you consider is essential information to get stakeholder approval of the project definition.

Everyone has their own ideas on what constitutes a definition but your purpose here must be to ensure that everyone understands:

❑ what you intend to provide from the project;
❑ what you do not intend to provide;
❑ when the outcomes are to be provided;
❑ what constraints you have identified;
❑ what risks are involved.

Is this what you have written down? Your purpose is to:

1. use the data gathered about customer needs and expectations;
2. turn these needs into requirements – what you believe satisfy the needs;
3. derive a project definition to specify these requirements;
4. ask your customer to approve this definition.

You can formalize the definition process using five essential documents. Don't waste time planning until these documents are agreed and approved by the customer and sponsor. The approval or 'sign-off' process is essential to maintain their commitment to your project. Now examine each of these documents.

Step 1: A project organization chart

Draw up a listing to show who is involved in the project, recording:

❑ name and job title/position;
❑ location;
❑ contact telephone/fax number and e-mail address;
❑ date assigned to the project;
❑ name of their line manager and contact data;
❑ distribution list.

Date the document and issue to everyone who needs to know – this is an essential communication document for resource planning. It ensures there is clarity about who is committed to the project.

Step 2: A statement of requirements

From the needs and expectations established in your discussions with the stakeholders, derive the data for this document. This must involve all the team to decide just what can be provided to satisfy the needs and may take several meetings. The document should record:

❑ needs and expectations identified and to whom attributed;
❑ how these needs can be met in practice;
❑ which needs cannot be satisfied yet and why;
❑ what assumptions have been made at this stage.

The statement must declare that it is based on available information at the date of preparation, as new data may become available later.

Step 3: A stakeholder list

As we discussed in Chapter 4, this list should exist and now you can formalize it for definition purposes, recording:

❑ name of stakeholder and job title/position;
❑ location and contact data (telephone/fax/e-mail);
❑ whether internal or external to your organization;
❑ ranking of importance to the project (high, medium, low).

Date this document because it is subject to change as you review the list at regular intervals. Ensure the list is distributed to all stakeholders.

Step 4: A project objectives statement

This information must be derived from working with your customer; it records:

❑ a statement of background;
❑ the project purpose – why are we doing this now?
❑ the overall project objective – in 25 to 30 words;

❑ the primary deliverables of the project with expected delivery dates;
❑ the primary benefits to be gained – preferably quantified financially;
❑ the cost of the project;
❑ what skills are required – particularly those not currently available;
❑ any identified interfaces with other active projects.

Ensure all deliverables and benefits satisfy the SMART test:

S pecific – clearly defined with completion criteria.
M easurable – understood metrics are available to identify delivery.
A chievable – within the current environment and skills available.
R ealistic – not trying to get the impossible with many unknowns.
T imebound – is limited by a delivery date based on real need.

It is also valid to identify any important aspects of your proposed strategy for the project, eg:

❑ examining several options;
❑ using sub-contractors for part of the work (where skills are missing);
❑ using consultants for support and advice;
❑ re-using known methods, processes or technology.

If preferred, this data can be included in the 'Scope of work statement'.

Step 5: A scope of work statement

This is a convenient place to record other useful data and cross-references to past reports and relevant projects. The document also includes:

❑ the identified project boundary limits – what you are not going to do;

❏ the standards and specifications that are applicable
  – internal product specifications
  – external product specifications
  – mandatory standards imposed by legislation
  – process specifications
  – customer specifications
  – standard operating procedures
  – purchasing procedures
  – quality standards
  – testing specifications and procedures;
❏ sub-contract terms and conditions imposed on third parties;
❏ any exceptions to these standards;
❏ where the standards and specifications are kept for reference;
❏ how success is to be measured;
❏ assumptions made.

The scope of work statement is a useful place to locate any other relevant information that supports and clarifies your defini-tion.

Step 6: A risk assessment

There are risks to all projects, and risk management is the process of identifying and containing them to ensure your project's success.
  What is a risk?

DEFINITION – A RISK IS. . .

any event that prevents the project realizing the expectations of your stakeholders.
A risk that happens becomes an issue that must receive prompt attention to maintain the project schedule on time.

A risk assessment at this stage of a project may kill the project, if it identifies such a high level of risk compared to other potential projects that it is not good business sense to continue. Three fundamental types of risks are always present:

1. *Business risks* – the viability and context of the project.
2. *Project risks* – associated with the technical aspects of the work to achieve the required outcomes.
3. *Process risks* – associated with the project process, procedures, tools and techniques employed to control the project.

As project manager it is your obligation, working with your team, to:

❑   identify and evaluate potential risks;
❑   obtain agreement to action plans to contain the risks;
❑   take the actions and monitor the results;
❑   promptly resolve any issues arising from risks that happen.

RISK ASSESSMENT

Why is it necessary?

You and your team will shortly start to plan your project and derive a schedule that is agreed with your customer. During the progress of the work many problems will arise, each potentially putting your schedule at risk. If the schedule slips there is always a reason. The risks that happen become the issues that you must promptly resolve to ensure the project schedule does not slip. This is shown in Figure 7.1. There is always the possibility of unforeseen risks leading to unexpected issues. Provided you react promptly you can still take the necessary actions to hold on to schedule dates. Identify the signals or triggers that suggest a risk is likely to happen and keep the team always alert to the possibility of any risk becoming a reality.

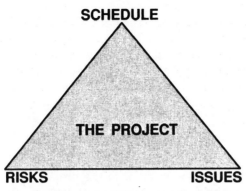

Figure 7.1 *Risk-issues-schedule*

When is it necessary?

Risk management is a *continuous process* throughout the life-cycle of the project and you must keep all the team focused on the risks:

❑ start now at the definition phase;
❑ it is essential to establishing the definition;
❑ compile a complete list as a 'project risk log';
❑ review the list at regular intervals as the project moves forward.

Review the project risk log at regular intervals, normally monthly at project progress meetings. Focus this review on:

❑ any change in the potential impact or probability of identified risks;
❑ any risks which have changed from previously lower ranking – these are then subjected to closer examination;
❑ deriving contingency plans for avoidance and/or damage limitation;
❑ adding any new risks identified to the list and assessing these for impact and probability.

Any risk entered on the list is *never* removed, even if the time zone when it could occur has passed. Your list of risks is a source of valuable learning data for future projects and is a useful data source for deriving checklists.

Assessing the risks

All projects have risks at the outset because of the many unknown factors, some of which you will remove during the planning stage. The risk could be due to external or internal factors. In practice risks disappear and new ones appear as the project progresses. Risk assessment requires answers to some key questions:

❏ What exactly is the risk?
❏ How serious is it as a threat to the project?
❏ What could be done to minimize its impact on success?

Call your team together and hold a brainstorming session to identify as many potential risks as possible – think of anything that could go wrong and hinder the project progress. Having identified all the risks, review the list, making sure none are repeated, then record them on a project risk log, giving each a number, name and the date identified. Then attempt to establish two characteristics for each risk:

❏ What is the probability of it happening – based on currently available data?
❏ What is the likely impact on the project if it happens?

This assessment can only be subjective, based on the previous experience of you and your team, but you should attempt to reach a consensus for each risk identified. Remember that *anything* that could go wrong and threaten the project is a potential risk and must not be ignored.

Ranking the risks

When you have derived your list of risks, use the team's experience to decide for each risk:

❏ the probability of occurrence on a scale of 1 to 9
   – 1 is low – most unlikely to happen
   – 9 is high – very high probability it will happen;

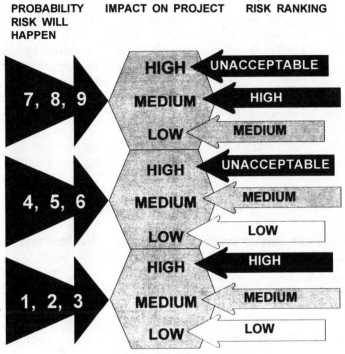

PROBABILITY   IMPACT ON PROJECT   RISK RANKING
RISK WILL
HAPPEN

7, 8, 9	HIGH	UNACCEPTABLE
	MEDIUM	HIGH
	LOW	MEDIUM
4, 5, 6	HIGH	UNACCEPTABLE
	MEDIUM	MEDIUM
	LOW	LOW
1, 2, 3	HIGH	HIGH
	MEDIUM	MEDIUM
	LOW	LOW

Figure 7.2 *Risk ranking*

❑ the impact on the project if it does happen
  – *high* – significant effect on the schedule and project costs
  – *medium* – less serious effect on the schedule, some effect
    on costs
  – *low* – some effect on schedule, little effect on costs.

Remember this should be a team consensus decision using all
the available information at the time. Once a set of risks has
been assessed for impact and probability of occurrence you can
rank them from Figure 7.2. Record the ranking on your project
risk log.

Continue to rank risks and review these rankings throughout
the project. The definitions are given below for high, medium
and low rankings:

High   Major impact on the project schedule and costs. Serious consequent impact on other related projects. Likely to affect a project milestone. Must be monitored regularly and carefully. Review action plans.

Medium   Significant impact on the project with possible impact on other projects. Not expected to affect a project milestone. Review at each project meeting and assess ranking. Monitor regularly.

Low   Not expected to have any serious impact in the project. Review regularly for ranking and monitor.

WHAT DO I DO NOW?

Any risks ranked as unacceptable must be closely analysed in more detail. If they could cause project failure, decide if some changes to the definition are necessary to reduce the level of risk. If you can do something immediately to reduce the ranking then you must derive and implement an action plan now. No project should really continue with such risks remaining. To derive action plans, record:

❏ a short description of the risk;
❏ when it is expected to occur;
❏ the probability assessed;
❏ what consequences are expected;
❏ what actions you propose to take if it happens;
❏ who will take the actions.

If you decide to change the ranking of a risk at any time, record the change and issue the updated project risk log to the stakeholders.

Once risks to the project have been identified and action plans derived, these must be monitored to make sure prompt action is taken when appropriate. We will consider this in the context of project control in Chapter 10.

CASE STUDY – SCENARIO 3

You have called the team together for a brainstorming session to assess the risks. As the meeting progresses, Janet seems to become increasingly negative about the project, saying that the risks are so great that the project shold be aborted now. This is having a negative effect on the rest of the team. You should:

1. Ignore the negative opinions and encourage the team to continue. Have a word with Janet after the meeting
   OR
2. Focus the team on the challenge ahead, reminding them that all projects have risks and it is everyone's responsibility to identify the risks and focus on avoiding them as much as possible
   OR
3. Close the meeting and continue the risk assessment without team involvement, making a decision to reconsider whether the negative team member should remain in the team.

A CHECKLIST FOR PROJECT DEFINITION

Ask:

- ❏ Is the project organization clearly established?
- ❏ Is the customer identified?
- ❏ Are roles and responsibilities at all levels understood and accepted?
- ❏ Have project accountability and authority statements been issued?
- ❏ Is the corporate and strategic context and priority of the project understood?
- ❏ Has a project organization chart been prepared and issued?
- ❏ Has the project stakeholder list been prepared and issued?
- ❏ Has a project need/purpose/opportunity statement been agreed?
- ❏ Has all the relevant background information been collected?

❏ Is there an agreed overall project objective statement agreed?
❏ Is there a business critical date for the completion of the project?
❏ Are the project deliverables clearly identified?
❏ Have the project benefits been established?
❏ Has the project approach and strategy been agreed?
❏ Is the project related to other projects?
❏ Have the project risks been identified and quantified so far?
❏ Has a project risk log been prepared?
❏ Has a scope of work statement been prepared?
❏ Have all assumptions made so far been documented clearly?
❏ Are existing communication procedures acceptable for the project?

GETTING YOUR PROJECT DEFINITION APPROVED

The final step in the definition process is to present your documented definition to the project sponsor and your customer for approval to go on to the planning phase.

Action Point

Ask the customer and project sponsor to sign all documents as approved, indicating their acceptance of the project definition you submit.

❏ Check that you have done everything necessary to fully and clearly define the project – use the checklist.
❏ Hold a meeting to explain any decisions you have taken following the earlier kick-off meeting.
❏ Show how all project documentation is to be kept secure and all documents display appropriate security classification codes.
❏ Explain how you intend to record project information and communicate with the stakeholders – set the ground rules.

Steps to Improve

1. Regard time spent on definition as an investment to save time later.
2. Clearly document your project definition as fully as possible.
3. Involve your team and any other appropriate experts in the process.
4. Carry out a risk assessment.
5. Rank and record the project risks for future review.
6. Get the definition signed as approved by the customer and sponsor.

8

Planning Your Project

Successful projects do not just happen: they must be planned. Planning is a process of creating order out of apparent chaos, made complex by the environment in which you are operating, continually facing change. Planning is just a process of asking questions:

What actions need to be done?
When are these actions to be done?
Who is going to do them?
What equipment and tools are required?
What is not going to be done?

Your purpose is to convert the contents of the project definition documents into a calendar-based plan of actions that everyone understands. This enables you to achieve the results on time, to the budgeted cost and to the desired level of quality. Project planning is carried out to:

❑ identify everything that needs to be done;
❑ reduce risks and uncertainty to a minimum;
❑ establish standards of performance;
❑ provide a structured basis for executing the work;
❑ establish procedures for effective control of the work;
❑ obtain the required outcomes in the minimum time.

You are rarely confident enough to plan all the detail work of your project at this stage. If the outputs from early work do not give the expected results, you have to take this into account to plan the detail of the following work. Planning is a dynamic and

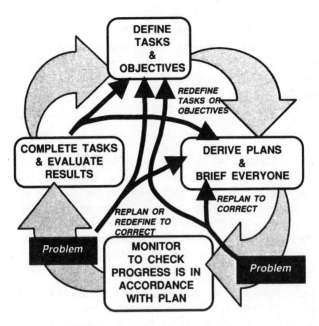

Figure 8.1 *The simple dynamic cycle*

continuous process to enable you to remain proactive through-out the project. You only finish planning when you finally close the project file (see Figure 8.1).

WHO NEEDS TO BE INVOLVED?

You and your project core team together. Planning is essentially a participative activity that contributes to team building and creates team 'buy-in' to the plans – this commitment is essential to success. Before you start your first planning session, review the skills and experience of the team members. If appropriate, invite experts from other departments to join you, stressing this is not committing them to project work later and that you value their inputs to your efforts. Persuade your project sponsor to attend and open the planning session, explaining the project strategic context, relevance and priority.

Do not derive a plan yourself and then seek agreement from everyone else – this would be a long process and one that does not create a sense of commitment in your team. It becomes 'your plan' and not 'our plan'.

CASE STUDY – SCENARIO 4

You have brought the team together for the first planning session, having told them last week of the meeting date, asking each to think about the project and the work they feel may be required. As you open the meeting, Graham tables a draft plan with all the key stages of the project derived and durations added to give the desired completion date. You are surprised but must now decide to:

1. Thank Graham for his efforts and ask the rest of the team to review the draft plan to seek a consensus view of its accuracy. Make a note to talk to Graham later about teamwork
    OR
2. Thank Graham but diplomatically set his plan to one side and ask each team member to develop their own plans for their part of the work for discussion at another meeting of the team tomorrow
    OR
3. Accept the plan and ask each team member to use it to develop their detailed parts of the plan within the fixed timescales of the draft plan.

WHERE DOES PLANNING START?

This is always subject to debate and argument. Should you fix the completion date and work backwards? Before going any further, some terms we use need defining:

SOME MORE DEFINITIONS. . .

A *task* – a (relatively) small piece of work carried out by one person.
An *activity* – a parcel of work of the project comprising several tasks, each of which may be carried out by different people.
Concurrent activities – activities (or tasks) that are designed to be carried out at the same time.
Series activities – activities (or tasks) that are designed to be carried out one after another, each strictly dependent on completion of the earlier activity.
Duration – the real time in working hours, days or weeks that a task or activity will take to complete.

Successful planning is a process of identifying sufficient detail to maximize concurrency and derive the shortest time to complete the project. You start by identifying the *key stages* of your project.

KEY STAGES

Identifying the key stages

Your need is to use the collective experience and knowledge of your project team and others invited to the planning session to identify the work as a list of activities (or tasks) to be done.

This is carried out in a brainstorming session. Write everything down on a flip chart, remembering to follow the basic rules of:

❑ quantity before quality – even if the same tasks appear more than once;
❑ suspend all judgement – disallow any comments.

The items are not ordered or ranked with any priorities at this stage and may seem to be a complete jumble from which no sense will ever appear. When everyone feels they have run out of ideas for tasks you can suspend the brainstorming activity. Then you can clean up the list by removing obvious duplicates and start to cluster those tasks that are clearly related.

Reduce your task list to a reasonable number of activities, preferably in the range 30 to 100 depending on the size of the project. These are the *key stages* of your project from which everything else is developed. The forgotten tasks lose significance for the moment as they are hidden away in the key stages and you can return to the detail later. This approach generally helps you identify most of the possible concurrency now and gives you an activity list that is relatively easy to manipulate. In practice your clustered list of activities will be at least 90 per cent accurate or frequently even better. Do give this process adequate time – it is an investment to save time later!

Using the key stages

Once the key stages are known and agreed you organize them into a logical sequence to maximize concurrency. There are some traps here for you:

❏ avoid considering real time or dates yet;
❏ avoid assigning people or functions to the key stages.

Both will lead you to create errors in the project logic.

The next step is to derive the *project logic diagram*. This is done using a technique known as 'taskboarding'. Write each key stage on a separate small card or notelet. Use these as parts of the project 'jigsaw' to build the picture. Arrange them in the right logical order, either on a table, using a white-board or simply use the office wall. This is achieved by taking each key stage in turn and asking:

What must be completed before I can start this work?

Start with the first key stages that begin from a card labelled START. Continue working from left to right until all the cards have been used. Connect them all with arrows to show the logical flow of the project from start to finish.

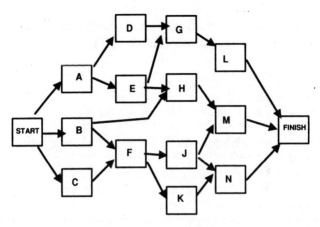

Figure 8.2 *Project logic diagram*

The advantage of this technique is that everyone can be involved. The visual impact of the diagram makes each member of the team question and debate the validity of the logic as it grows.

Note that the logic diagram is continuous, ie, every key stage has at least one arrow entering (an input dependency) and at least one arrow leaving (an output dependency). To assure integrity of the logic, this rule must be maintained otherwise the plan will contain errors. Of course it is not unusual to find more than one arrow depicting dependency entering and leaving some key stages.

Note also that a fundamental property of the diagram is that a new activity can not logically start until all immediately previous activities finish. If you find on reviewing the logic that a following key stage can start earlier than the end of the previous key stage, the latter must be split to show that earlier dependence.

Keep a record of all the dependencies you have agreed. You may input this information to project management software later to prepare the schedule. When recording dependencies only record each immediate predecessor key stage for any particular key stage.

A CHECKLIST FOR DERIVING THE PROJECT LOGIC DIAGRAM

❑ Time flows from left to right.
❑ There is no time scale on the diagram.
❑ Place a start card/adhesive note at the extreme left of the sheet.
❑ Place a finish card/adhesive note at the extreme right of the sheet.
❑ Prepare a separate card/adhesive note for each key stage.
❑ Start each key stage description with a verb (present tense).
❑ Do not attempt to add durations for the key stage yet.
❑ Use different colour cards/adhesive notes for different functional activities, if appropriate.
❑ Locate the cards/adhesive notes on the sheet in order of dependency – debate each one.
❑ When all the cards/adhesive notes used, validate the dependencies – try working back.
❑ Show the dependency links as finish to start relationships initially.
❑ Do not take people doing the work into account – this can produce errors.

THE PROJECT WORK BREAKDOWN STRUCTURE

The work breakdown structure (the WBS) is a means of graphically presenting the work of the project in a readily understandable format.

The project key stages form the highest level of the WBS which is then used to show the detail at the lower levels of the project. You know that each key stage comprises many tasks identified at the start of planning and later this list will have to be validated. Expanding the WBS to the lower levels, as shown in Figure 8.3, is the process of multi-layer planning you use throughout the project.

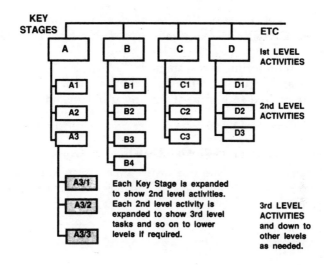

Figure 8.3 *WBS*

Note that:

❏ The WBS does *not* show dependencies, just a task grouping under each key stage.
❏ It is not time-based – there is no time scale on the drawing.

ALLOCATING RESPONSIBILITY

Each of the key stages of the project needs to be owned by one of your team members. This allocation of responsibility is essential to make sure the work is done on time and your objective is to fairly and evenly distribute the work in the team. You must persuade each member of the team to accept the role of *key stage owner* (KSO) for one or more key stages.

The KSO accepts the obligation for his or her key stage to confirm:

❏ the work required is identified at the detailed task level;
❏ the dependencies are clearly identified;
❏ the estimates of durations are accurate;

❏ the work gets done on time to the quality needed;
❏ the work conforms to quality procedures and requirements;
❏ regular monitoring is maintained;
❏ regular and accurate status reports are issued;
❏ you are alerted promptly about any problems and issues.

Action Point

Each key stage can only have one owner even if that person assigns
some of the tasks involved. Split or multiple ownership leads to
confusion and no ownership.

Ensure your team members have:
❏ a strong sense of commitment to the project;
❏ the tools for the job;
❏ the essential environment for quality to be maintained;
❏ access to the right skills for the work;
❏ the visible support of yourself and the project sponsor;
❏ a clear understanding of the performance expected of
them.

Allocating responsibility is not a matter of random choice or an
auction: you must heed the current circumstances of each
individual.

It is almost certain that your project team members have other
non-project work to do, or even work on other projects. You
must ensure this other work is taken into account when
allocating responsibilities or you will force people into overload
and increased stress levels. Some people can not say 'No' and
you must be confident that responsibilities are taken seriously.

Record your allocated responsibilities

Keep a record of the responsibilities you have allocated. This is
a key communication document for everyone involved, including the line managers of the people assigned to the project. As

the plan develops, more names are added as the extended team is identified for parts of the detailed work. Your responsibility chart should record:

❑ a list of the key stages, and for each –
   – who is responsible
   – who should be consulted for advice
   – who must be kept informed of progress
❑ and later add –
   – planned start date
   – planned finish date
   – whether a critical activity.

Your reason for allocating these responsibilities is to assign the estimating of key stage durations to those people in your team who are most likely to have the appropriate experience or know who to consult to get the experienced inputs.

ESTIMATING

What is an estimate?

An estimate is a decision about how much time and resource are required to carry out a piece of work to acceptable standards of performance. This therefore requires you to establish the 'size' of the task or group of tasks, determined from measurements if possible, and the amount of 'effort' required to complete the work. Ask:

❑ How can the work be broken down?
❑ Can it be divided between two or more people?

Effort is measured in project time units – hours/days/weeks. Once the effort is known then optimize the resource needs, taking individual available time into account to determine the amount of effort required from each. Effort is a direct measure of a person's time to do a piece of work in normal work days. Unfortunately that person will often have other non-project activities to complete which reduces their capacity to do the work. At a capacity of 50 per cent the work will take at least double the number of work days. In practice it takes longer because of the 'back-track' effect due to the breaks in the flow of the work. Effort is a measure of continuous work with no interruptions.

Duration is a conversion of effort taking into account the number of people involved, their capacities and an allowance for non-productive time. Since duration is measured in real working days, this is never the same as the schedule, which has to take into account:

❑   days not available for project work;
❑   non-working days – weekends;
❑   public and organization holidays;
❑   staff holidays.

The first step for you is to calculate some realistic durations and then apply these to a calendar to derive a schedule.

Estimating the durations

As the duration of each key stage is the real time it will take to complete the work, this is usually the most difficult part of the planning process. Unfortunately there is an abundance of 'good advice' in most organizations about how long a piece of work will or should take. The sources for accurate estimates are limited:

❑   the experience of others;
❑   the expert view;
❑   historical data from other projects.

There is no substitute for experience. If similar work has been done before, you can ask those involved for their advice and adjust the data for your project. It is a reasonable way to start, but be cautious: the equation relating *effort* and *performance* is different for us all.

Who are the experts? There may be a few – or so they believe! Always ask questions about how reality compared with original estimates for some work. Check that the nature or content of the work did not change. You soon discover who is above average at estimating accurately. Keep a record of how the estimates are derived in case they are wrong, then you can improve your estimating skills.

People problems of estimating

Ask anyone how long a piece of work will take and you are likely to be given a shrug and a smile and a wildly inaccurate answer. This is because they do not ask themselves some simple questions:

❑ Do I really understand what is involved?
❑ Do I have all the necessary skills and tools for the work?
❑ What else must I do at the same time?
❑ What is the priority of the project work over other work?
❑ When is it really needed by?
❑ Can I break the job down into chunks to do at different times?
❑ Can I predict what I will be doing when this project work needs to be done?
❑ Will I be taking any holiday during the time concerned?
❑ Do I have any other obligatory commitments during the time concerned?
❑ What does my manager know about my future commitments that I do not know yet?

The reality is that the majority of people are not productive 100 per cent of the time! As much as 20 per cent of the working week is taken up by:

meetings	general interruptions
visits to desk and others	equipment failure
reading journals and e-mail	searching for information
giving support and advice	unforeseen events
seeking advice from others	communication failures
personal organization	engaging in conflict
inability to say 'No'	others.

Consider also:

❑ project complexity;
❑ specifications – adequacy, unfamiliarity;

❑ new quality standards;
❑ unclear understanding of the technology;
❑ new technology – a learning curve for confidence;
❑ team size and location of the team members, etc.

The answers to these and other similar questions are often ignored in deriving an initial estimate, leading to considerable problems later.

Contingencies

The purpose of contingencies is to attempt to quantify the extent of uncertainty in the estimating process that makes up the project plans. Contingencies are not intended to cover changes to the project definition or objectives after they have been agreed with the stakeholders. Remember that most people include their own contingencies to protect themselves when asked for time estimates!

Agree the durations to be inserted in the plan with the team. From these, calculate the total project time with a projected completion date. Obviously there is a balance between the desired project completion date and the projected or forecast completion date based only on estimates. Somewhere in the middle there is an acceptable solution and only attention to detail and all the experience you can gather will help you to find it.

Time-limited scheduling and estimates

There is always a conflict when a completion date is imposed on a project before any work on estimates is carried out. This imposed date is outside your control completely, so you would have to try and compress estimates to fit the plan. To a limited degree this is acceptable as a target but too often this process moves you into a totally unreal situation where you are faced with 'Mission Impossible'. You must still prepare realistic estimates to derive a clear case and state:

❑ What you can deliver in the time.
❑ What you can not deliver in the time.

❏ Why you can only meet part of the objectives of the project.

You can then use your skill as a negotiator to arrive at an agreed solution!

GUIDELINES FOR ESTIMATING

Schedule full-time team members at three and a half to four working (productive) days per week, to allow for holidays, absences, training courses, etc.

❏ Include management time where appropriate as an additional 10 per cent.
❏ In planning, avoid splitting tasks between individuals.
❏ When tasks are split between two individuals do not reduce the time by 50 per cent – allow time for communication and coordination.
❏ Take individual experience and ability into account.
❏ Allow time for cross-functional data transfer and responses.
❏ Build in time for unscheduled urgent tasks arising on other non-project activities.
❏ Build in spare time for problem solving and project meetings.

Any estimate is only as good as the data upon which it is based so, like project risks, accept they may change with time as more data becomes available to you. For each key stage keep a record of:
– the estimates you have finally decided;
– any assumptions made during estimating;
– where contingencies have been added ;
– how much contingency has been added.

IDENTIFYING THE CRITICAL PATH OF YOUR PROJECT

Critical path techniques have been in use on projects now for some 30 years, having proved their value as a tool for project scheduling and control. The fundamental purpose is to enable you to find the shortest possible time in which to complete your project. You can do this by inspection of the logic diagram.

Enter the durations on to your cards in the logic diagram for each key stage. Begin at the 'start' card and trace each possible route or path through the diagram to the 'finish' one, adding the durations of all the key stages in the path. The path that has the highest number, ie, the longest duration, is the critical path of your project and is the shortest time to complete the project. All other paths are shorter. All the key stages on the critical path must, by definition, finish on time or the project schedule will slip.

This is where reality hits you – is the project total time what your customer actually requires? If it is a long way out, do not worry yet as most project managers expect this to happen. Remember your estimates are based on people's perceptions. Your job is to attempt to compress the schedule to a time that is both real and achievable and satisfies your customer. To do this you need to make use of another valuable tool of project management – Programme Review and Evaluation Technique (PERT). This tool allows you to analyse the logic diagram to confirm:

❑ the critical path – confirmation of your inspection;
❑ the start and finish times of all the key stages;
❑ the amount of 'spare time' available in the non-critical key stages.

All this information is very useful to you for optimizing the project schedule, but more importantly for the control of the project work once this starts.

The PERT critical analysis technique

The PERT method of critical path planning and scheduling is the most commonly used technique for project management control. It is based on representing the activities in a project by boxes (or nodes) which contain essential information calculated

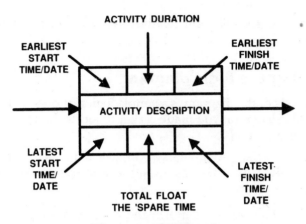

Figure 8.4 *PERT node*

about the project. The interdependencies between the activities are represented by arrows to show the flow of the project through its various paths in the logic diagram. The PERT diagram (sometimes referred to as a 'network') is identical to the logic diagram you derived earlier, each card/adhesive note for a key stage representing a node.

The conventional data stored in the node box is shown in Figure 8.4. The four corners of the node box are used to store the four characteristic times for the key stage. These are calculated times using the durations derived in estimating – remember to keep all durations in the same units.

The default or normal relationship used is finish to start. Under certain circumstances it is valid to impose constraints with the start to start or finish to finish relationships between activities, ie, pairs of activities are forced to start or finish together. You can impose a forced delay using a *lag* between the start or finish of a predecessor activity and the start or finish of one or more successor activities. The forced start or *lead* is used to start a successor activity before the predecessor activity is completed.

Lags and leads should be used with care – it is easy to become confused and introduce errors. Split an activity instead of using leads to keep the diagram relatively easy to read and understand.

Analysing the logic diagram

The analysis of the diagram is a simple logical process extending the initial calculation you made earlier to locate the critical path. Two steps are involved:

1. Adding durations from start to finish – the *forward pass.*
2. Subtracting the durations from finish to start – the *backward pass.*

The calculations are not complex and the step-by-step process is given in Appendix 2. In this way you and your team can quickly calculate the total project time and find those areas of the project where float or spare time exists.

Using the PERT analysis data

At this point in the planning process you may be looking at a plan that is giving you a total project time considerably longer than you really want. Do not despair – yet! Do not allow yourself to be tempted to go back and amend your time estimates. The next step is to convert the PERT data into a graphic format that is easier to work with and understand. This is the Gantt chart – a very useful tool for project work originally devised by Henry Gantt early in this century. An example is shown in Figure 8.5.

The chart is divided into two sections, a tabulated listing of the key stages and a graphic display where each key stage is represented by a rectangle. All the rectangles are located on a time-scaled grid to show their position in the schedule. It is useful to have both a project time-scale bar and a calendar time-scale bar across the top of the chart. This allows you to include the non-working days such as weekends and holidays. The key stages are listed on the left-hand side by convention, in order of their occurrence in the logic diagram (working from left to right).

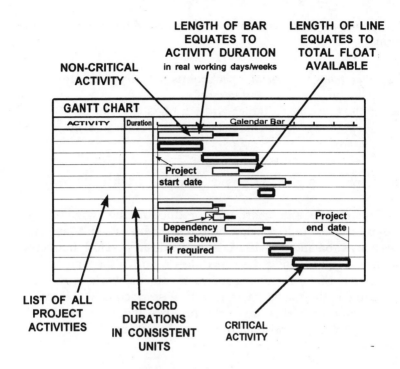

Figure 8.5 *Gantt chart*

You will note that the float time is also shown on the chart as a trough extension to those rectangles or 'bars' (the common term) on the right-hand end, ie, at the finish end of the bar. When you initially draw any Gantt chart the float is *always* drawn at this end. The limit of float is the limit of the time available if the schedule is not to be threatened and the whole project extended.

Of course critical activities have zero float and you can choose to highlight these. You can include the dependency arrows on the chart between the start and finish of the dependent activities (ignoring the float zone).

The Gantt chart can also include some other useful information:

❏ *Milestones* – special checkpoints usually indicated by a triangle or a diamond symbol.
❏ *Project meetings* – indicated by a filled circle or dot.
❏ *Project reviews* (ie, financial/audit) – indicated by a filled square.

Remember to give a legend describing what the symbols mean!

The initial Gantt chart you produce at this stage is then optimized to reflect what you can achieve with available resources balanced with customer desires. This frequently involves compressing the schedule to reduce the time for the project. If there are no resources to do the work in the time scheduled, the Gantt chart is a useless document expressing hopes and wishes! Analyse the resource requirements for the tasks in the plan and then optimize the schedule.

Does a computer help?

These steps may involve considerable reiteration to arrive at an acceptable solution – a process where project management software is very powerful. Small changes in the schedule are rapidly reflected in the chart and the logic simultaneously recalculated automatically. This allows you to carry out a 'what if' analysis, viewing the impact of changing anything in your plan in a host of different ways. You can explore all available options you can think of to derive a finally acceptable schedule.

This process is necessary to convince your customer and the project sponsor just what is realistically possible if clear commitments of resources are made. Obviously this process is much more time-consuming if carried out manually!

CASE STUDY – SCENARIO 5

Your team is having some difficulty laying out realistic schedules to meet the customer's expectations. You are being asked many questions and they seem to be approaching the scheduling in the right way but are having trouble coming to consensus decisions. The detailed planning is taking much longer than you expected, so you should now:

1. Leave the team to carry on with their work and eventually come to a conclusion as they will learn from the experience
   OR
2. Give the team your ideas on how to resolve their problems and hope this will encourage their own creativity and lead to effective schedules
   OR
3. Participate in the work yourself and facilitate the planning until an acceptable schedule is derived.

ANALYSE YOUR RESOURCE REQUIREMENTS

Ask your key stage owners to validate the task list in their respective key stages using the techniques applied earlier for the key stages. Much of the data will have already been generated, but this now needs some closer analysis, particularly for the initial key stages. Identify the people most likely to be assigned to the work and then, working with them as an extended team:

❑ review the initial task list;
❑ add to the tasks where necessary;
❑ analyse for the 'often forgotten tasks'
  – documentation
  – approval times

- testing, planning and development
- project reviews and gathering the data
- project meetings, replanning and planning reviews
- customer meetings and user group meetings
- negotiations with suppliers
- expediting and administration.

Suggest each key stage owner:

❑ derives a complete list of tasks in their key stage;
❑ produces a responsibility chart for each key stage;
❑ estimates the durations of all the tasks in the key stage;
❑ identifies the actual people who will carry out the work;
❑ confirms their commitment and availability.

Remind the team that when identifying resources they need to review:

❑ previous experience   ❑ individual capabilities
❑ technical knowledge   ❑ accuracy of their work
❑ speed of working   ❑ capacity to do the work.

Use the same techniques as before to derive the logic diagram for all the tasks inside each key stage. Then determine its critical path and the total float available in the tasks. Some of these tasks may be assigned milestone status later. This enables you to produce a Gantt chart for each key stage. In this way a detailed plan of the work for a particular part of the project is clearly defined by the people doing the work and it minimizes misunderstandings about responsibility.

You now have the data to update the WBS. However, another advantage of this method is that the detailed work of a key stage does not need to be derived until a week or two before the work starts. This allows the planning to incorporate any unexpected outputs from earlier key stages. In this way you continuously work to hold your plan dates, seek the required resources, validate your estimates and optimize your schedule to meet the total project time desired.

OPTIMIZING YOUR SCHEDULE

The schedule is always based on the calendar, taking into account the non-working days during the project. It involves taking decisions by consensus to maintain a balance between:
- the schedule – time;
- the resources available – cost;
- performance – scope and quality.

The options available are fairly limited when optimizing trade-offs between these three to arrive at a solution. There is no perfect plan, only the best solution based on available information at the time. The options are:
- re-evaluate the dependencies in the logic for the key stages;
- review relationships – initially you used finish to start, now examine if other types give an improvement;
- introduce lags and leads – with caution though;
- split key stages to get more concurrency;
- review assigned durations – review any contingencies added;
- review original estimates – realistically;
- seek more or different resources;
- seek to get current resource capacities increased – more time available;
- examine to ensure reinvention is minimized;
- reduce scope, quality or specifications – a last resort option.

Float time is not to be seen as an opportunity to stretch an activity to fill the available time. If you allow this to happen you create another critical activity by convention, so it is easy to turn everything critical by using up all float.

Action Point

Tell your team that float time is only used as a last resort with your consent (during the execution phase) to enable recovery planning when things go wrong.

When you are confident you have a realistic acceptable schedule, update the key stage Gantt chart. Check your original project definition to ensure you have not ignored anything – particularly expected dates quoted and assumptions made.

Present this schedule informally to your customer and project sponsor to confirm if it is acceptable. If it is not, then you must seek alternative solutions through further optimization. If the schedule is nominally agreed you can proceed to the final steps of planning before launching the actual work.

REVIEW YOUR PROJECT RISK LOG

Review all the risks identified during the project definition phase. Ask:

❑ Have any changed status?
❑ Are there any new high risks? Identify actions on a risk management form.
❑ Are there any new risks identified from planning?

Examine your plan to identify possible risk areas:

❑ tasks on the critical path (and inside a key stage);
❑ tasks with a long duration (low capacity factors?);
❑ tasks succeeding a merge of two or more activities in the network;
❑ tasks with little float left (where is the float?);
❑ tasks dependent on third parties;
❑ lags and leads;
❑ start-to-start relationships;
❑ tasks using several people (particularly at different times);
❑ complex tasks;
❑ anything involving a steep learning curve;
❑ tasks using new or unproved technology.

Prepare new action plans for any new high risks identified or those that have moved up in ranking. Assign responsibilities for day-to-day monitoring of risks to the key stage owners. Stress the importance of monitoring for the triggers that could signal a risk becoming an issue. Avoiding a risk is better than a damage limitation exercise later!

REVIEW YOUR PROJECT BUDGET

Begin by updating the project WBS with all the lower level detail – or at least as much as you can at this stage. This is the easiest way to work out the cost of each based on:

❑ capital equipment costs;
❑ resource direct costs – based on cost rates;
❑ revenue costs for the project team – materials, expenses, etc;
❑ indirect costs – chargeable overheads, etc.

With the costs of each key stage identified you can produce an operating budget – the real budget for project control purposes. If it varies significantly to the original approved budget you were given by the project sponsor then this variance must be investigated and the conflict resolved. If an increased cost is identified, then the customer will need to be consulted for approval. Prepare for this discussion by deriving some alternate options as you did when optimizing the schedule earlier. Keep a record of all costs for control measurement and variance analysis as your project proceeds.

FREEZING THE BASELINE PLAN

Review the plans you have now derived and make sure you have not forgotten anything! The plan which is soon to be frozen is the baseline plan. Everything that happens in future will be measured against this plan. You will need to present the plan documents to your sponsor and then the customer for approval and acceptance. Use the checklist to review the plans with the team and ensure you have not forgotten anything.

A BASELINE PLAN CHECKLIST

Ask:

❏ Is the project definition still completely valid?
❏ Is the scope of work statement still valid?
❏ Has the project manager's authority been confirmed in writing?
❏ Are all stakeholders identified?
❏ Does the team understand who manages the stakeholders?
❏ Is the WBS developed as far as practicable?
❏ Does the WBS include all project administration tasks?
❏ Are customer and sign-off checkpoint meetings included?
❏ Is the critical path established and agreed?
❏ Are all key stages allocated for responsibility?
❏ Are key stage owners clear about their responsibilities?
❏ Is the project risk log complete and up to date?
❏ Are estimation records in the project file?
❏ Are resource loadings and capacities optimized and agreed?
❏ Does the Gantt chart reflect an agreed plan and schedule?
❏ Has the project operating budget been derived and approved?
❏ Does the team include all the skills needed?
❏ Has action been taken to acquire unavailable skills needed for the project?
❏ Are team members working well together?
❏ Have any conflicts been resolved promptly and effectively?

Add additional questions to ask as appropriate.

SEEKING APPROVAL TO LAUNCH YOUR PROJECT

You have now completed the planning phase as far as necessary before launching the project work. At this point plan documentation comprises:

❏ a list of key stages;
❏ the project logic diagram;
❏ a project key stage responsibility chart;
❏ responsibility charts if appropriate for each key stage;
❏ a record of estimates for all the key stages;

❏ an optimized project Gantt chart for the key stages;
❏ Gantt charts for the early key stages or, if possible, for all of them;
❏ an updated and reviewed project risk log;
❏ a project operating budget.

Present these documents to your customer and project sponsor for signature of approval to proceed.

Steps to Improve

1. Involve the team in the planning activities.
2. Invite additional support from appropriate experts.
3. Ensure you give enough time to deriving the logic.
4. Clearly allocate responsibilities for project activities.
5. Estimate durations with care and avoid over-optimism.
6. Familiarize yourself with the PERT analysis technique.
7. Optimize your schedule to a realistic level avoiding over-compression.
8. Always review the project risks at regular intervals.
9. Seek approval of your plans before launching the project.

9

THE PROJECT LAUNCH

After all the hard work of defining and planning the project the euphoria of getting agreement with your customer can quickly evaporate if you don't keep up the momentum.

There are still a few things to think about before you hit the 'go' button. You cannot continue with the work based on just promises of resource availability. You need to take such statements a stage further to be sure resources are available to you just when the plan tells you they are required and that you will not be let down!

Are you really confident? The key stage owners for the early key stages should have identified all the tasks to be carried out in each. This task list is the basis of ensuring you get the commitment you need.

HOW CAN I CONFIRM RESOURCE COMMITMENTS?

Ask the key stage owners to verify their task lists, making sure they have not forgotten any tasks. If appropriate, get them to work out the logic diagram for the key stage using the same techniques you used earlier. Issue a standard format to record these task lists with a clear identification of who is responsible for completing each task in the key stage. It is also useful to record:

❑ the key stage code as recorded on the WBS;
❑ the key stage schedule start and end dates, whether it is critical, and calculated float;

❏ the duration of each task in the key stage, using consistent units;
❏ the amount of float in each task, if this has been calcu-lated;
❏ the plan start and end dates for each task;
❏ a record of the *actual* start and end dates for each task.

Once the work plan is complete, confirm that all the tasks are:

❏ allocated to someone for responsibility;
❏ have plan start and end dates;
❏ are realistic and achievable within the total time planned for the key stage without using the float time.

The document is signed by the key stage owner, yourself and the line manager of the people being committed. This sign-off also allows you to verify that the task list does not:

❏ include tasks that you do not want done or consider unnecessary;
❏ omit some tasks that you consider essential to your pro-ject;
❏ have any obvious estimating errors.

Copy the work plans produced in this way to the people involved and their line managers. This reminds them of the contract they have entered into. If the result is not acceptable, optimize the schedule using the same approach that you used when deriving your original Gantt chart. Your choices are limited but usually enough to come up with a satisfactory and acceptable solution:

1. seek more resource capacity;
2. obtain more resources;
3. review and modify the logic inside the key stage;
4. amend the scope or quality of the work.

Although this may seem to be a time-consuming activity, you are only asking your team to use a consistent and disciplined approach to work planning. You do not need to produce all the work plans at the outset, just those for the first few key stages. As the project continues, you can work proactively to prepare more work plans, taking into full account everything that has happened in the project. This is known as 'layering the plan' as the project proceeds. It is more effective and less time-consuming, minimizing replanning of detail due to changes.

If the logic diagrams for each key stage are worked out, turn these into individual Gantt charts to produce a family of charts at the second level of planning aligned with your overall key stage Gantt chart.

CASE STUDY – SCENARIO 6

The second phase of the project is a significant proportion of the work involving several people in a particular department. They have been closely involved in planning this phase. The manager has sent you a memo asking for your performance evaluation of all his staff assigned to do project work. Your team have been working closely with these people, so you should:

1. Respond promptly and point out that performance issues are part of his or her job, not yours
   OR
2. During your one-to-ones with team members, make this an additional responsibility for them and seek their evaluations for your report
   OR
3. Call the team together and tell them of the request. Then work together to evaluate each individual assigned and agree what to report.

ESTABLISHING A MILESTONE SCHEDULE

Recall the earlier diagram relating the schedule to risks and issues. Replace 'schedule' with 'milestones', since these are all the significant events that are due to occur during the execution of the project. The milestone is a flag or signal at some clearly

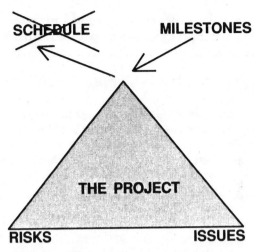

Figure 9.1 *Milestone schedule*

defined point in the project. That signal indicates that something special should have happened or is about to happen. The milestone is a point of control, placing target points in the project schedule for certain events to be signed off as completed.

Some of the common events given the status of project milestones are:

❑ completion of a key task, eg, providing output to third parties;
❑ completion of one of the project deliverables;
❑ stage generation of benefits;
❑ completion of third party significant event, eg, acceptance tests;
❑ completion of third party activity, eg, delivery of equipment or data;
❑ a financial audit point;
❑ a project audit point;
❑ a quality audit;
❑ completion of a significant stage of work (possibly a critical element);

❏   a significant decision point, eg, abort the project;
❏   completion of a project stage to release further funding.

DEFINITION – A MILESTONE IS. . .

a significant, measurable event in the project life-cycle.
Think of the milestones as the 'marker posts' to show the route
to the finishing post – project completion. For a successful
project you must reach each milestone on time or explain why a
slippage has occurred.

Ask each key stage owner to suggest the milestones in their key
stage and agree these in a team meeting. The frequency of
milestones in a network must be sufficient for effective control.
Record the list of milestones on a schedule and on the Gantt
chart. For effective control *all* milestones must be measurable
with clearly established metrics – apply the SMART test you
used with deliverables earlier.

ENSURING EFFECTIVE COMMUNICATION

Poor communication is a major source of conflict and slippages
so give this serious attention before you start the project work.
Ask yourself:

❏   Who needs to know?
❏   What do they need to know?
❏   How much do they need to know?
❏   How often must they be informed?

Establish distribution list(s) as appropriate but avoid generating
large volumes of paper. Decide the ground rules you will
impose on everyone to get prompt feedback on the prevailing
situation with the work in progress. Effective monitoring and
tracking of the project is dependent on good communication in
the team, between you and the team and your key stakeholders.
You need prompt feedback about:

❏   current progress of the active tasks;
❏   problems encountered with the work;
❏   problems anticipated with work waiting to be done;
❏   technical difficulties being encountered.

Control in a project environment requires you to have a continuous awareness of what is happening and what is due to happen next. Promptly identify any problems that interfere with progress. Potential changes to the plan must be brought to your attention. Lay out the ground rules for an early warning system – it can save a great deal of re-work later and reduce the risk of replanning. Stress that you are always willing to make time available to discuss difficulties and give help and guidance. This effectively means you:

❏   are always ready to listen to their concerns and difficulties;
❏   want regular verbal reports and documented progress reports;
❏   want to be informed promptly of any risks identified;
❏   need to be told if anyone anticipates a problem or risk occurring, however trivial it may appear to be.

Continually reinforce the need for good communications and create a climate that encourages regular sharing of information in the interests of continuous improvement. Evaluate performance openly, not to blame when things do not go according to plan but to learn and improve performance.

PROJECT STATUS REPORTS

Your key stakeholders expect to receive regular status reports. Decide the frequency and format of these with your customer and sponsor. Define any jargon clearly and ask yourself just what you need to know about the status of the project, such as:

❏   what has been completed;
❏   what has not been completed and why;
❏   what is being done about the incomplete work;
❏   what problems remain unsolved;

❑ what needs to be done about these unsolved problems;
❑ what difficulties are anticipated in the work waiting to be done.

Tell the team how you want these reports given, and their frequency. It is appropriate to design a single page standard template for reporting project progress to ensure consistency and focus. This template should record:

❑ a concise summary of overall progress;
❑ a list of milestones due to be completed since the last report and their current status, ie, on time or late;
❑ a list of milestones with dates due in the next reporting period;
❑ actions set in place to correct any slipped milestones;
❑ forecasts for the project completion based on current information;
❑ reasons for any revision to earlier forecasts to completion;
❑ changes to the project risk log;
❑ any issues (problems) outstanding still waiting for resolution.

No one likes to hear bad news, but the sooner it is exposed the quicker you can react to limit the damages and take corrective action. You can use this template at any level in the project – the key stage owners reporting to you and your reports to the customer and sponsor. Good teamwork is directly related to effective and regular communication.

WHAT MEETINGS DO I NEED?

You must now decide what meetings are essential to the project process. Consider:

❑ one-to-one meetings with the project sponsor;
❑ one-to-one meetings with your team members;
❑ project progress meetings with the team;
❑ problem-solving meetings;
❑ meetings with particular stakeholders – the customer;

❏ project review meetings with the stakeholders.

All are necessary at different frequencies throughout the project and all must have a clear purpose. The one-to-one meetings are very important to maintain close contact with your project sponsor and the members of your team, helping you to:

❏ know and understand these people as individuals;
❏ give and receive information at a personal level;
❏ discuss problems of a more personal nature that impact on performance;
❏ give guidance and support;
❏ coach team members;
❏ recognize their efforts;
❏ encourage and support personal development.

This creates a motivating climate in your team, encouraging open communication and sustaining the focus on the project's success. Set up a schedule in your diary for regular one-to-one meetings (say monthly) with each team member. Decide with your project sponsor how often you should meet and diarize these meetings. Allow about 30 minutes for each one-to-one discussion.

Problem-solving meetings tend to be held as problems arise, involving specific people, which may not mean the whole team. Do not mix problem-solving with progress or team meetings as the discussion easily gets out of control and the meeting becomes diverted from the purpose.

Agree a schedule of project progress meetings, throughout the whole project, showing the schedule dates on the key stage Gantt chart. If you have nothing to discuss, cancel or postpone any meeting. Weekly short meetings at the start or end of a week are good for small to medium sized projects if all the team are on the same site. If your team is multi-site the frequency is likely to be monthly, so open other communication channels where appropriate – e-mail or video link meetings.

Project review meetings with your stakeholders are less frequent and usually involve you in preparing much more material to present formally to the group.

HANDLING PROJECT CHANGES

That sinking feeling – uncontrolled change! However good your plans, there are certain to be some unexpected surprises. Minor changes appear during monitoring and are controlled by prompt action and taking corrective measures. Significant change is much more serious and needs closer scrutiny. These changes can come from the customer, the end-user, the sponsor, or from technical problems. All can lead to replanning of the project and modify the objectives. Any change that is expected to create a replanning activity and affect the total project time as currently scheduled must be handled in a formal manner. Always examine:

❑   the source of the change request;
❑   why it is necessary;
❑   the benefits from making the change;
❑   the consequences of doing nothing at this stage;
❑   the cost impact of making the change;
❑   the effect on project constraints;
❑   the effect on resource needs;
❑   any increase or decrease in project risks;
❑   the effect on the objectives and scope of the project.

Major change can have a demotivating effect on the team unless it is something they have sought in the interests of the project. A major change on one project could have serious impact on the resource availability for another project. All major change must be approved by the customer and the project sponsor before action is taken to replan. Derive alternative solutions and examine the consequences and risks before seeking an agreement with the customer. Design a standard template to formalize change requests – this often makes many potential changes suddenly disappear!

HOLD A LAUNCH MEETING

Now you can launch the project. The final steps after completing the baseline plan include:

❑ preparing work plan for the early key stages;
❑ deriving a milestone schedule for the project;
❑ deciding a progress reporting process with the templates everyone must use;
❑ deciding a change management process with appropriate templates;
❑ agreeing a meetings schedule.

This launch meeting is a milestone in your project after which all project work starts. Collect together all the important people who are involved with your project and explain the plans in some detail. Prepare yourself and your team well for the meeting. This is an important opportunity for you to explain the plan and the areas of high risk to achieving success. You are looking for acceptance from all those present that the project is well planned. You must convince them that with their cooperation you can achieve the objectives. No one can later complain they do not understand the project plan or what you are trying to achieve. It is an ideal opportunity for team building. The chances of getting the team and stakeholders together in a project are rare and this meeting helps them understand their responsibilities in an organizational context. Make it a special occasion and provide some lunch – if your budget allows!

Steps to Improve

1. Develop good relations with all your resource managers.
2. Ensure detailed planning at lower levels of the WBS is complete.
3. Secure resource commitments and explain the project plans.
4. Set the project milestones and record them – stress their importance.
5. Carefully design your communication and reporting needs.
6. Ensure the team understand their responsibilities for reporting to you.
7. Set up a process for handling significant changes.
8. Hold a project launch meeting.

10

CONTROLLING THE WORK

Planning activities are fun and somehow not real work because the outputs are easily changed and there are no consequences other than more paper! No one feels threatened by the situation because they are not measured for performance in the same way as when the real work of the project starts.

There is sometimes an 'adrenalin dip' when the team feels they should be doing something but nothing appears to happen. Immediately after the launch meeting, call the team together for a very short team meeting. Give encouragement and:

❏ reinforce the motivational level in the team;
❏ check that there are no concerns or misunderstandings;
❏ confirm everyone is clear about the initial, scheduled work;
❏ remind them:
  – to tell you if any problems occur
  – to watch out for new risks
  – to report signals that suggest a risk is likely to happen
  – to report any issues promptly
  – that your door is always open to discuss problems.

HOW DO I COPE WITH NEW INFORMATION?

New information inevitably comes in to the team members after the work starts. This can be quite casual, through informal meetings in the corridor, staff restaurant or even the car park, or from lower level sources in the customer's organization. The input is also intentional on occasions and could have profound effects on the work, the schedule and team motivation.

You must prevent any input amending the plans, creating more work than necessary; remind team members to inform you immediately of such situations. You are asking your team to keep you informed of progress, so when additional information appears you, and the team members, must ask:

❏ Where does the information come from?
❏ Why was it not exposed before?
❏ Who has decided it is relevant now?
❏ Is the information accurate and realistic?
❏ Is there some hidden agenda associated with the timing?
❏ What impact does it have on the plan and schedule?
❏ Does this change the project objectives, deliverables or benefits?

Project work can be seriously constrained, or even sabotaged by the subtle transfer of erroneous information to a team member. A complete absence of information when it is due to appear can have similar sinister origins. Always be openly prepared to consider changes to your plan when essential. If the information essential to the project work is confused by mixed messages from different people then you face potential conflicts and confusion. Prepare your team for these events because they are certain to occur at some time in the project's life – if you have not experienced them already!

Your early warning system is the best way to get feedback about what has happened and what needs to happen. This provides you with the information to control the project.

WHAT IS CONTROL?

Control of a project environment involves three operating modes:

❏ *Measuring* – determining progress by formal and informal reporting.

❏ *Evaluating* – determining cause of deviations from the plan.
❏ *Correcting* – taking actions to correct.

Control is associated with the present, so reporting is time-sensitive to allow you to take prompt corrective action. If all reporting is historical and a considerable time after the event, then you cannot control your project. The communication processes you established during the project launch are designed to give on-time visibility to significant events.

DESIGN YOUR CONTROL SYSTEM

The purpose is to ensure that you and the team always have the information to make an accurate assessment of progress and keep the project under control. An example is shown in Figure 10.1 below.

The best control system is the simplest. The basic inputs to control are the plan and the actual results observed and

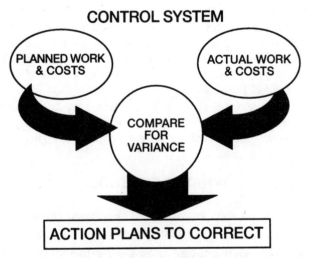

Figure 10.1 *Control system*

measured by the team. The comparison activity should show whether the project is on track and everything is going according to plan. If this is the case, you can update the project records and charts and report progress to your customer and project sponsor. To control the project you must use problem-solving techniques to prepare and implement an action plan to correct the difficulties and restore the project to the planned schedule.

It is essential to measure the impact of action plans to provide feedback in the system and a check that the solution has worked. Controlling the project means managing the many problems that arise to maintain the project schedule through:

❏ monitoring the work – observing and checking what is happening;
❏ identifying and resolving the issues that arise;
❏ tracking the project – comparing with the plan and updating the records.

The simplest way to track your project is to use specific control points – the project milestones. Focus the team on these marker points, stressing the importance of maintaining the dates and that you must know if any milestone date is expected to slip. Remind them that the total float is not spare time for them to use by choice without reference to you. Keep the project file up to date with a regular check and update of:

❏ the organization chart;
❏ the stakeholder list;
❏ the key stage responsibility charts;
❏ the key stage Gantt chart;
❏ the work plans;
❏ the project risk log.

Depending on the size of the project, you can speed up the administration process using a project management software package – once you are familiar with its many features!

Keeping the project file up to date is an obligation you must fulfil. You could be moved to another project at any time and someone else has to take over. Do ensure that the legacy you leave behind is a good one, otherwise you will continually be subject to queries and requests that interfere with your new role.

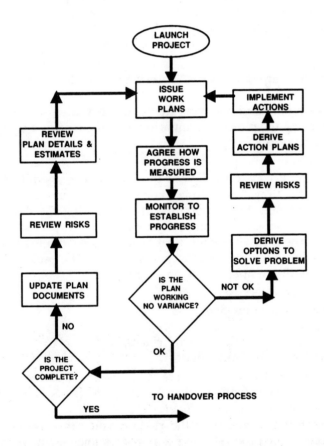

Figure 10.2 *Monitoring system*

MONITORING PROGRESS

You cannot do this effectively from behind a desk – you need to walk about, observe and have conversations! This is your data-gathering process which, if done effectively, is far more useful then any written report. Confidence in progress reports only comes from verifying these from time to time. This obliges you to monitor:

❏   the team;
❏   the stakeholders;
❏   performance.

Monitoring is a checking activity to:

❏   talk to the team members to find out directly how things are going;
❏   encourage the team and show you care about them and their work;
❏   check that promised resources are in fact working on project tasks;
❏   rapidly learn about concerns and difficulties.

Too much monitoring may sometimes be perceived as inter-ference, so there is a fine balance to be struck.

Decide the frequency

Do not rely on team meetings as the focal point of reporting project progress. You must decide how often you intend to:

❏   walk about to observe what is happening – daily?
❏   hold one-to-one meetings with the customer, the project sponsor and the team members;
❏   measure progress of key stage tasks and milestones;
❏   receive local reports – verbal and written from key stage owners.

If possible, have regular short team meetings at the same time and day each week. This encourages the team to share information and maintain good communication with each other. Regular monitoring demonstrates your concern for success and reinforces messages about watching out for new risks or anticipating future problems.

How is progress measured?

Ask the team how progress is easily measured. They must agree:

- ❏ how to set output criteria for each activity;
- ❏ the performance metrics to use and confirm completion;
- ❏ the frequency of measuring and recording;
- ❏ how to report the progress and deviations or exceptions.

If unusual or unexpected results appear you need to be informed promptly so that corrective action can be decided. Continue to remind the team to watch out for the risks that are particularly relevant at each stage of the work.

HOW CAN I MANAGE THE ISSUES?

The purpose of an issue management process is to make sure all risks that happen are resolved promptly to avoid and/or limit damage to your project. Let us be clear what we mean by an issue:

DEFINITION – AN ISSUE IS...

any event or series of related events (that may have been previously identified as a risk) that have become an active problem causing a threat to the integrity of a project and/or related projects.

Managing issues is similar to managing the original risks, requiring you to keep records of all issues that occur and ensure action planning is promptly used to resolve the issues.

Your primary concern is to get an action plan in place and implemented. It is too easy to over-react and action the first solution you come up with. This is not always the best solution and ignores the team's expertise in deriving an answer to the problem. Keep a record of all significant issues as they happen, giving:

❑ issue name and source;
❑ who owns it;
❑ which parts of the project are affected;
❑ who is responsible for action plans to resolve;
❑ a record of current ranking;
❑ when action is complete.

Design a template similar to the project risk log. Issues are identified through regular monitoring.

Should issues be ranked?

Since you have limited authority it is unlikely you can resolve all the issues without support from your sponsor. Ranking an issue clearly identifies who is responsible for deriving the action plan. Issues raised are ranked according to their impact and anticipated consequences by assigning a red, yellow or green flag:

Red flag: major issue having serious consequences for the project. Prompt action needed to implement a decision to resolve.
Responsibility: Project sponsor.

Yellow flag: significant impact on the project and/or other projects. Unless resolved promptly will cause delays to milestones. Becomes **red** if action delayed more than two days.
Responsibility: Project sponsor.

Green flag: consequences limited to confined area of the project and unlikely to impact other projects. Becomes **yellow** if not resolved in time to avoid project slippage.
Responsibility: Project manager.

Outstanding issues are identified when reporting progress of the project. You must also ensure that the ranking of any issue has not changed. It is important to keep your key stakeholders informed on progress with resolving issues, invoking their active support when necessary in the interests of the project.

CASE STUDY – SCENARIO 7

The customer unofficially informs you that he has a problem and this could result in some changes to the requirements. This could spell disaster for your project. The customer has asked for a meeting within the next week at your office to discuss the details. To prepare for this formal meeting, you should:

1. Call an immediate meeting of the team and ask them to prepare an agenda for the meeting, identifying the items to discuss
    OR
2. Ask the team to improve productivity before the meeting as this should impress the customer and show you are doing a good job
    OR
3. Ask all the team to ensure all their reports and project records are accurate, complete and updated and prepare status reports for all key stages of the project
    OR
    Is there another action you would consider?

Resolving issues

Remember that issues interfere with your target of maintaining the project schedule so, apart from prompt reaction, make sure that you:

❑ involve the team in solving problems;
❑ use additional expertise where appropriate;
❑ identify areas of the project affected:
   – consequences as perceived now
   – consequences in the future if not resolved
   – options to resolve the problem and, for each option:
     cost and resource implications
     effects on the project schedule
     effects on scope – quality
     risks associated
     future issues identified.

Always confirm that responsibility is clearly allocated for actions planned to avoid confusion when action is implemented:

❑ Who is responsible?
❑ When must the action be completed?
❑ Who must be kept informed of progress?
❑ Who monitors – during and after?

TRACKING YOUR PROJECT

Tracking is the process by which the project progress is measured through monitoring to ensure that:

❑ changes to the plan caused by issues or the customer are promptly acted upon;
❑ the reported progress information is used to update the plan charts and records in the project file.

To do this you must have a starting point or baseline against which the variances are identified. The baseline for all tracking is the project plan devised before implementation, where all key stages are fixed.

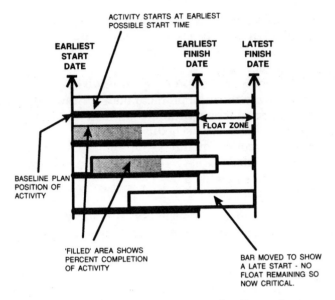

Figure 10.3 *Current status on the Gantt chart*

The project baseline should remain unchanged throughout the project. As the work is done you mark progress on the chart by filling in the bars to show the amount of work completed.

If a key stage is late starting, takes longer to complete or the finish suffers a delay, this is shown clearly on the chart. The original position of the bar on the chart is unchanged as the baseline.

Modifications to the plan are recorded as they occur to enable the experience to be logged for future projects. This may move one or more activities away from the original baseline position, modifying the project strategy. Keeping the baseline unchanged forces you to fully document any changes to the plan and schedule and later evaluate the key learning points from all these changes that occur.

If any of these modifications cause a slippage to critical key stages, then the project completion will be delayed. You then face the difficult task of recovery planning to restore the original project schedule or persuade the customer to accept the extended completion date.

Deciding what completion means

In project work you must sometimes take a ruthless approach to completion because it is frequently difficult to clearly define what we mean.

The bar on a Gantt chart is a linear graphical representation of effort. In real life effort is never linear and depends on:

❏ the accuracy of the detailed planning of tasks to do;
❏ the complexity of the work;
❏ the amount of interruptions to the work;
❏ the availability of data and equipment;
❏ how the individual feels on the day.

The well-proven 80/20 rule applies – 80 per cent of the results come from 20 per cent of the effort and the remaining 20 per cent of the results takes 80 per cent of the effort! There are nearly always forgotten tasks that take a significant amount of time to complete:

documentation	approval times
developing test procedures	project reviews
project meetings	planning reviews
replanning meetings	customer meetings
user-group meetings	negotiations with suppliers
expediting	searching for information
purchasing and administration	training
travel and communication	updating project records.

Don't ask for 'per cent complete' assessments when seeking progress data. You need to know whether the task will finish on time, so ask for a forecast of when it will be completed. This focuses the individual responsible for the work on reviewing other commitments due in the same period and giving a more realistic assessment of the time to complete. If the forecast completion date is then clearly unacceptable, take some prompt corrective action. You should persuade all your key stage owners to get into the habit of forecasting performance for their key stages. Forecasting:

❏ improves everyone's ability to estimate time to do the work – forecasting is a 'real time' activity, not looking into a crystal ball for the distant future;

❏ creates real targets for the individual doing the work – any delay beyond an agreed target cannot be tolerated.

Ask for regular reports, along with reasons for any changes to previous forecast completion dates. Encourage the team to develop expertise in accurate forecasting to expose potential future variances. The analysis for variances at all stages must be a primary concern for the whole team, making sure effective corrective action is taken when any issues occur.

Taking corrective action

Analysis of a variance should help to expose the causes of the problem. Your primary concern is to maintain schedule integrity – no slippages. Taking corrective action usually has limited possibilities:

1. Rearranging workload(s) if a milestone date is going to be missed – find others to take on some of the tasks to relieve the loading, or even reallocate the tasks to others who can work faster.

2. Put more effort into the job – not an easy option to demand in practice as everyone is probably feeling overloaded already.

3. Put additional resources on to the job – resource constraints may negate this option, but as a short-term measure you may find some extra help for a few days.

4. Moving the milestone date – subject to the stakeholder's approval and time recovery later in the project; difficult with activities on the critical path. Recovery of time later is always at the expense of something.

5. Lower the scope and/or quality of the results demanded by the plan – only possible with the agreement of the customer and it will take considerable negotiation.

Corrective action is normally approached using these options in this order, remembering all could have a cost implication. Record any assumptions you make when deciding action plans – they could be significant later!

Before deciding which option to use, check if:

❑ the critical path has changed;
❑ any individual workload is adversely affected;
❑ any milestones are subject to slippage;
❑ any new high risks are exposed;
❑ any new issues are exposed;
❑ any cost over-runs are introduced – do these need approval?
❑ any localized schedule slippages are controllable.

CASE STUDY – SCENARIO 8

You have completed the first phase of the project and the results and outputs were not quite what you expected. This affects the estimates for the next phase and highlights that your original estimates were too optimistic. You are now facing a probable slippage of two weeks to the project completion date. Your customer is not going to be happy about this, so you must:

1. Ask the team to meet and seek some way of improving their productivity for the next phase, hoping they will come up with a solution
   OR
2. Ignore the slippage at this stage. These problems occur in project work and eventually sort themselves out. You feel you can still motivate the team to meet the completion date
   OR
3. Call a team meeting and emphasize that this is a crisis for the project. Work with the team to review the estimates and the project logic to find a way to restore the scheduled completion date.

Progress reporting

For good control you must check your communication processes are working and providing the right information. If they are not working well then agree with the team how to improve them. Check with your customer and the project sponsor that they are getting all the essential information they need. Avoid creating an enormous paper trail. Keep reports short using templates, but expect to make a more detailed presentation occasionally at a full project review. Focus the reports on the project milestones:

❏ short summary of progress;
❏ milestones due and completed;
❏ milestones due that have slipped;
❏ corrective actions put in place because of slippage;
❏ milestones due in next reporting period;
❏ issues escalated and waiting for decisions;
❏ new issues escalated;
❏ forecast of project completion;
❏ reasons for any revision of previous forecasts.

Project control is dependent on good communication and feedback. Keep the process working to avoid confusion and misunderstandings.

Update the project file regularly

Write everything down to remember! The project file is a source of all relevant information, current and historical, about the project and must be comprehensively maintained. This includes all latest issues of standardized records including those held on computer systems. Do not rely on the integrity or availability of computer records alone. Refer back to Chapter 6 for the suggested file contents. Remember the project file is a living record of the project and becomes an invaluable source of data for future projects.

Remember the project log book?

If you opened a project log book at the start of the project, use it as a daily diary of events in the project. Always keep it with you and record events as they happen. The information you note here will help during the evaluation process after hand over to the customer.

Progress meetings

Regular progress meetings are an essential part of the project control process to review the current status at any time. Take specific actions to make them effective. Everything that has happened before the meeting is ancient history! Remember that time spent in a meeting is time lost to project work, so:

❑ keep your status meetings short – maximum one hour;
❑ keep meetings to the point and focused on exceptions;
❑ avoid diversions;
❑ start and finish on time;
❑ maintain good control;
❑ have the updated key stage Gantt chart available for reference;
❑ identify the outstanding issues but do not try to solve them in the meeting – set up a separate discussion with the relevant people.

Focus the team to ask:

❑ What has been completed on time?
❑ Any outstanding exceptions to the work done?
❑ What actions agreed earlier are incomplete?
❑ When outstanding action plans will be complete?
❑ Which milestones are completed on time?
❑ Which milestones have slipped?
❑ Are action plans in place to correct slippages?
❑ Any risks escalated to issues?
❑ Issues still waiting to be resolved?
❑ Any resource capacity changes forecast?
❑ What work is to be done in the next period?
❑ Which milestones are due in the next period?
❑ What problems are anticipated in the next period?
❑ Any risks that could affect the work in the next period?

❏ Any problems anticipated with third party contracts in the next period?
❏ Any team performance problems and issues?

Always have a flip chart stand in the meeting room and record agreed actions on the sheet as they occur, with responsibility and target completion date. In this way there should be no doubt in the team who is responsible for which actions and they do not have to wait for the minutes. Avoid:

❏ long verbal reports of what has been done;
❏ problem solving in the meeting – take serious issues off-line;
❏ long debates – they detract from the purpose and cause deviation;
❏ negotiations – usually excludes most of those present;
❏ any other business – the biggest time-waster!

The action list is the most important document to come out of the meeting and this is the starting point of the next meeting – checking all agreed actions have been completed.

CASE STUDY – SCENARIO 9

You are three-quarters of the way through the project. You have accepted some earlier customer changes and rescheduled the project to everyone's satisfaction. You now receive a call from the customer asking for an assessment of the consequences of cancelling the project immediately. It is stated that another project is planned and you may be given the job. You should:

1. Decide not to involve the team at this stage as the work is progressing very well. You have had these scare messages before and nothing has resulted. Review the consequences yourself
   OR
2. Call the team together, expose the request and assess the risks and possible consequences, stressing that work must not be suspended as these things often happen
   OR
   Is there some other action you can take?

HOW DO I CONTROL COSTS?

Control of your project is not just about controlling the effort and work outputs, but should also involve cost measurement. To demonstrate success you must not exceed the budget. In many organizations the only way you can have accurate and up-to-date information on how much you have spent is to do it yourself. Once you make a commitment to spend some money in your project, it is out of your budget. Unless the accounting system records this commitment the finance report will not show this potential cash outflow until an invoice appears several weeks or months later. The budget report still shows you have more money left than is really true!

Accurate cost control is only effective if *all* costs are measured, including the costs of people working on the project. This means everyone must record their time spent on project work so that this can be costed. Cost rates often include all indirect costs such as rents, heating, lighting, etc for the organization. If the time data is not collected in a consistent and disciplined way, then you cannot control the costs very accurately. Your monitoring process must therefore include accurate measurement of:

❑ the time spent on each task;
❑ the resources used on all tasks;
❑ cost of materials (and wastage) used;
❑ cost of equipment time used;
❑ capital expenditure committed;
❑ revenue expenditure committed.

Normally you make these measurements over a specific period of two or four weeks or by calendar month. Alternatively you must resort to applying cost rates to the planned resource allocations. This assumes that what actually happens is exactly as planned. As we know this is not true, you must adjust the costs for each activity based on actual start and finish dates.

For effective control you need information on:

❑ the project budget, a cumulative total divided into accounting periods;
❑ the costs incurred in the current accounting period;

❑ the costs incurred to date from the start;
❑ the work scheduled for completion according to the plan in the current period;
❑ the total work scheduled for completion to date;
❑ the work actually completed in the current period;
❑ the total work actually completed to date.

The WBS is the essential budget building tool to derive a costing. Measure costs incurred as the work proceeds and compare with this budget.

Cost control measures

Four essential measures are used for the control of project costs:

BAC – Budget at completion. This is based on the operating budget developed from the WBS for the whole project.

BCWS – Budgeted cost of the work scheduled. At any specific time the schedule shows a certain amount of work should be completed. This is presented as a percentage completion of the total work of the project at that time. Then: % Scheduled Completion × BAC = BCWS.

BCWP – Budgeted cost of the work performed. At any specified time the actual work measured as complete is compared with the scheduled amount and the real percentage completion calculated. Then: % Actual Completion × BAC = BCWP. The BCWP is the earned value of the work completed.

ACWP – Actual cost of work performed. At any specified time the actual cost incurred for the work. The timing of the actual cost measurement coincides with the percentage completion progress measurement so that the actual cost can be compared with earned value (BCWP).

Other terms often used include:

FTC – Forecast to complete. A forecast of the cost to be incurred to complete the remaining work. This may be an extrapolation using an analysis model or simply the best estimates of all the costs to complete the project.

CV – Cost variance. The difference between the value of the work performed and the actual cost for that work. ie, CV = BCWP − ACWP. If the actual cost is above the budget, the CV becomes negative!

SV – Schedule variance. The difference between the value of the work performed and the value of the work that had been scheduled to be performed, at the same measurement point in time, ie, SV = BCWP − BCWS. If the work done is behind schedule the SV becomes negative! The variance measures are often used for trend analysis, because of their sensitivity to changes as the project progresses.

How can I record cost data?

The most accurate way is to tabulate all data using a spread-sheet programme on a computer to calculate and update the data at regular intervals.

This makes it easier to incorporate any amendments to the budget resulting from major changes to the project. Most spreadsheets include charting features and the data is then used to automatically generate a chart showing the progress of the BCWP, and ACWP against the BCWS as the project progresses. Keeping your own records of costs also ensures it is regularly updated. It provides you with data to compare with financial budget reports issued from other sources.

Steps to Improve

1. Carefully design your control system.
2. Ensure the team understands the importance of communication.
3. Set up regular team meetings to review status.
4. Review plans and estimates, adjusting as required.
5. Review the project risks at regular intervals.
6. React promptly to issues and plan actions to correct.
7. Focus everyone on maintaining milestone dates as a commitment.
8. Stress the importance of cost control and keep records.

9. Keep the project file updated regularly.
10. Maintain your visibility with the team.
11. Operate an open door policy – be available to guide and support.
12. Ensure stakeholders receive regular reports of progress.

11

PROJECTS AND CONFLICT

Conflict and change are partners, never far apart, so accept the inevitable and be prepared to react when necessary. Your project involves many different people all with their own hopes, desires and needs. These differences lead to conflict and when such differences surface they are often seen as difficult, troublesome, annoying or even embarrassing and an intrusion into a calm and ordered life.

A large part of your time can be occupied with fighting the fires and crises evolving from conflicts.

WHY DOES CONFLICT OCCUR?

Many conflicts arise from situations where roles and responsibilities are not clearly defined, leaving the team members confused. Some common causes are:

❏ diverse expertise in the project team;
❏ low level of authority given to the project leader;
❏ lack of understanding of the project objectives by the project team;
❏ excessive role ambiguity in the team – unclear or shared responsibilities;
❏ unclear schedules and performance targets for team members;
❏ infringement of functional status and roles by project processes and procedures;

❏ remote functional groups operating almost independently on project work;
❏ local interference from high-level management involvement;
❏ people just don't like each other or get on together in their work.

Most conflict arises from the way people behave with each other in a particular situation and unfortunately behaviour is not predictable.

IS CONFLICT GOOD OR BAD?

Conflict is good if it:

❏ brings problems and issues out into the open for discussion;
❏ brings the team together, increasing loyalty;
❏ promotes creativity, generating new ideas and work practices;
❏ focuses people to give their work more detailed analysis.

Good conflict generates a win-win relationship between individuals, promoting sharing of information and improved motivation.

Bad conflict:

❏ creates stress, stirring up negative feelings;
❏ makes the working environment less pleasant;
❏ severely reduces the effectiveness of communication processes;
❏ interferes with coordination of effort between groups and individuals;
❏ encourages an autocratic approach to working.

Bad conflict tends towards a win-lose relationship developing between individuals. You need to create a climate in the team where conflict is seen as healthy and valued for the results created. A team with no conflict could be perceived as complacent and lethargic with little creativity.

TYPES OF CONFLICT

The most common types involve one or more of the following:

❏ resources;
❏ equipment and facilities;
❏ budgets and costs;
❏ technical opinions and trade-offs;
❏ priorities;
❏ procedures;
❏ scheduling and estimating;
❏ responsibilities;
❏ personality clashes.

Personality conflicts are often the most difficult to deal with and may only be resolved finally by total separation of the parties.

CONFLICTS AND RISK

Many of the conflicts that occur can be predicted as potential events in a preliminary risk assessment. Resource allocation and prioritization between several active projects or other operational work is frequently a source of conflict, particularly as priorities are changed to satisfy external pressures. Examples of risks that can become a source of conflict include:

❏ unclear objectives and project definition;
❏ project priorities versus other work not exposed;
❏ resources not available when promised;
❏ delays in interfaces with other projects downstream;
❏ changes in the scope of work and project parameters;
❏ technical disagreements in innovation.

Conflict can hinder project progress and even lead to the wrong or undesirable results. Regard conflict as an issue to be resolved as quickly as possible to avoid serious consequences.

CASE STUDY – SCENARIO 10

Your team has taken a very optimistic approach to the project schedule. Some line managers have refused to support these schedules. Your team expected to be involved in discussions to optimize the schedules and reach a mutual agreement. You feel you might need to get involved and should:

1. Ask the team to meet and discuss ways to resolve the conflict and derive possible solutions. Stress you are available for advice if necessary
    OR
2. Meet with the line managers to understand why they have rejected the schedules then call a special team meeting and resolve the conflict by changing the schedules
    OR
    Is there another option?

HOW CAN I MANAGE CONFLICT?

Any temporary management situation produces conflicts. This naturally results from the differences in the organizational behaviour of the individuals involved who all come from different functional groups.

You operate in an environment of constant and rapid change. The functional manager works in a more standardized and predictable environment. Recognize the gap between these two environments so you can react appropriately when a conflict occurs. There is no single method of managing all conflicts in such temporary situations. Try to:

❏ anticipate their occurrence;
❏ understand their composition –
   – Why has a conflict occurred?
   – What is the background?
   – Who is involved?
   – Who is affected?

❏ assess the consequences for –
  – teamwork
  – the project work
  – the schedule.

Remember people's behaviour directly contributes to conflict. Constantly look for possible areas of conflict in the same way as project risks are regularly reviewed. Most people are reasonable and if you maintain everyone's focus on the project objectives the conflict can be seen in perspective. If people in conflict do not resolve their differences between themselves, then you must intervene in the interests of the project. Then you are faced with:

❏ imposing a solution – that neither person likes;
❏ invoking a third party to arbitrate;
❏ negotiating;
❏ reducing the conflict in importance in favour of another issue;
❏ using the rule book or policy statements to break the conflict.

Conflict rarely goes away on its own, so ignoring it only adds to your problems. Your team expect you to deal with such issues promptly in the interest of good teamwork and you risk losing their trust and respect if you just avoid them.

Steps to Improve

1. Don't ignore conflict – it often sticks.
2. Maintain a constant watch for conflicts arising.
3. React promptly to conflict that impacts on project performance.
4. Encourage creativity and teamworking.
5. Identify real sources of conflict, not just the perceptions.
6. Use risk assessment to predict possible conflicts and build action plans to avoid.

12

ENCOURAGING EFFECTIVE USE OF TIME

As time always moves inexorably on it is natural to assume things are happening according to the plans. The reality is often far from expectations, not because the plans are wrong but due to poor time management. Some people are very skilled at organizing and managing their time. For those not so organized, their work output is extremely vulnerable.

Performance is directly related to effort which yields an output and these results are dependent on how well an individual makes the best use of time. You have a direct interest in how everyone working on even the smallest part of your project is using the time allocated to the actual work. Your stake obliges you to:

❏ influence how time is used;
❏ avoid unnecessary work;
❏ avoid duplication of effort;
❏ ensure attention is given to prioritizing the work.

Time is your most valuable resource which if lost or misplaced, is gone forever. For you it is therefore a constraint and you must encourage everyone involved to use effective time management principles to maximize this resource.

The most significant problem with people and time management is actually recognizing and accepting that there is a problem. Once it is recognized as such, it can provide an opportunity to develop effectiveness, reduce stress and improve the probability of success for your project.

Ask yourself some questions:

❑ Do you have trouble completing work to deadlines?
❑ How long can you work at your desk before being interrupted?
❑ How long can you work at your desk before interrupting yourself?
❑ How many interruptions (typically) occur each day?
❑ Have you a procedure for handling interruptions?
❑ Can you set aside a large block of time for something important?
❑ How much overtime do you work to get the job done?
❑ How is incoming mail handled?
❑ How much time do you spend attending meetings?
❑ How tough is it to say no?
❑ Do you carry out work you could allocate to team members?
❑ Do you make a fresh 'To Do List' every day?
❑ Is your list prioritized?
❑ How do you approach detailed work when it is necessary?
❑ Do you have flexibility in your diary for reactive time?
❑ Is your routine work made easier with established procedures?
❑ Does the team understand your time management principles?

Making time a manageable resource requires you to think carefully about these questions. As you are almost certainly doing some of the project work yourself, the barriers to effective time management affect you just as much as your team members.

CASE STUDY – SCENARIO 11

You are becoming increasingly concerned about Ian's performance, which seems to be deteriorating. He is a very quiet, almost introverted type and you are unsure whether he has a personal problem or is finding the work pressure too high. You should:

1. Call a team meeting and open a discussion about how performance and productivity is not as good as at the outset. Ask the team to derive some ideas for action to improve things
   OR
2. Do nothing for now. It may be a personal problem which will work itself out and performance will be restored to recover any lost time
   OR
3. Have a one-to-one discussion with Ian and try to get him to see his own performance issue. Try to help him understand the real cause and how to derive a solution.

BARRIERS TO EFFECTIVE TIME MANAGEMENT

If you spend too much time doing project work yourself, you will be robbed of valuable time to control the project. If you are unable to say no you quickly become burdened with everyone's problems. Common time-robbers include:

Poor communication
Uncontrolled visitors
Too many meetings
Casual conversations in office
Record-keeping
Changes without explanation
Procrastination
Too much attention to detail
Unclear objectives
Lack of project tools
Bureaucracy
Strong functional boundaries

Unclear responsibilities
Lack of information
Too many project reviews
Tracing data and information
Changing priorities
Unnecessary crises
Executive interference
Over-commitment
Lack of support
Confirming resources
Politics and power games
Arson – creating crises.

You can probably think of many more, all influencing you to some degree, and many having a serious impact on your effectiveness. The consequence of these time-robbers is a reduction in the working day for you and your team.

WHAT CAN I DO?

Start by addressing some fundamental issues. You cannot hope to encourage others in your team to improve their time management if you display all the symptoms of hopeless disorganization. Use your time effectively by:

❑ Allocating work clearly to the team members.
❑ Limit your own assigned work in the project schedule.
❑ Don't take on more than you really know you can complete on time.
❑ Consult as required, but take decisions promptly and explain them.
❑ Prepare your own 'To Do List' and *update every day.*
❑ Set your own priorities and generally stick to them.
❑ Focus on the areas of high risk in the currently active project work.
❑ Do the difficult tasks first or when you can concentrate most effectively.
❑ Control the project work by exception, reviewing the plan charts each day.
❑ Avoid wanderlust – monitor effectively when necessary.
❑ Focus everyone on the project objectives.

Regularly ask yourself some simple questions:

❑ What am I doing that really does not need doing?
❑ What am I doing that someone else could do just as well or even better than me?
❑ What am I not doing that will not get done at all if I avoid doing it?
❑ What have I done to establish clear priorities and targets for me and my team?

❑ Have I confirmed that everyone clearly understands what is expected of them?
❑ Have I communicated the current priorities to everyone who needs to know?
❑ Does everyone know and understand the consequences of ignoring the priorities?
❑ Is everyone aware of the high risk areas and the triggers to identify potential issues?

The answers will lead you to improve the way you use time and encourage others to adopt the same process.

Steps to Improve

1. Examine how you use your time now.
2. Identify where you waste time – measure it with a time-log.
3. Prioritize the work by importance to the project.
4. Avoid unnecessary re-work.
5. Ensure all responsibilities are clearly understood and priorities agreed.
6. Encourage your team to openly discuss time management problems.
7. Give active support and guidance to the team on using time effectively.

13

WORKING IN A MATRIX

Most of the projects in an organization are carried out using people in different departments, divisions or even from different sites and countries. How can you possibly hope to manage the team member's effective use of time and maintain your project schedule in such an environment?

The short answer is, 'with great difficulty and a risk of increased stress levels', although there are some actions you can take to help make everyone's life more comfortable. Many of the problems arising with a project team drawn from the organizational matrix focus on time issues.

WHAT CAN I DO?

Step 1: Keep the stakeholder list up to date

Pay particular attention to the line managers of all the resources you are using or plan to use in the future. These people hold the keys to success. Your ability to influence them will be continually tested to ensure the project work is always started and completed on time.

Keep them well informed of the project progress. Agree with them how the work is to be broken down into tasks, and remind them of the consequences to the business if the project suffers a slippage.

Step 2: Monitor to minimize 'back-tracking'

When the project file is opened to start a piece of work there is inevitably a need to review what was done the last time on that particular item. If it was several days before, then there is a need to go back over what was done and achieved. The time for this 'back-track' is often significant, especially when you add up the number of times it happens in a project. Going back over previous work may lead to a complete review and amendment of earlier work, which might be beneficial occasionally but is often unnecessary re-work.

Step 3: Agree project work is done in reasonable 'chunks'

Try to get agreement that project work is always given a sufficiently large chunk of time to achieve some specific measurable output without any interruptions. Changes of priority are inevitable in departments you do not control. Try and get line managers to enter into firm commitments that your work will not suffer unnecessarily if crises occur – they are often an excuse for lack of progress.

Step 4: Encourage your team members to set priorities

Give support and guidance when appropriate. Satisfy yourself that the time allocated is adequate to complete the work on schedule. Remember everyone is different in the way they work and in their pace. Encourage the team to expose and discuss their project work priorities with their line manager so that interruptions can be minimized and time used effectively. This helps the line manager to control and map their departmental resource utilization.

Step 5: Set personal targets for each member of the team

These are effectively the dates created in the project plan, but alterations are often caused by the changing priorities and minor slippages of earlier work. You must continually review these targets and take into account the slippages and the actions implemented to correct the time lost. The plan is dynamic and must be regularly updated to reflect these changes, and the information must be distributed to everyone involved.

Step 6: Continually reinforce feedback and reporting

Do not allow slippages to go unreported to you and the line manager. Missed targets push your project into fire-fighting mode. Try and keep proactive, continually monitoring future resource loadings and commitments so you can assess the impact on your project. This will minimize the incidence of unforeseen risks and you can use 'what-if' analysis with the Gantt chart to decide corrective actions to keep everything on track.

The most significant cause of failure in a matrix-type project is poor communication. Misunderstandings are usually due to poor listening and unclear communications with little or poor back-up documentation. Use the milestone schedule as a means of communicating to everyone the key dates which must not be missed and check that everyone understands their obligations to meet these dates. Continually reinforce communication feedback processes that keep you informed of issues arising that impact on milestones.

CASE STUDY – SCENARIO 12

At a regular progress team meeting it becomes apparent that one particular department is having difficulty meeting deadlines. Data and reports eventually get issued but usually late and this is frustrating the team. It appears that all documentation is being channelled via the manager's desk, leading to hold-ups. This manager has a reputation for such behaviour, insisting she sees everything leaving her department. She has apparently caused this problem on other projects over the past three years and insists on running her department this way. You should:

1. Set up another team meeting later the same day to find ways of obtaining the project data and reports without interfering with the departmental policies
   OR
2. Ignore the issue and treat it as a common and normal difficulty of project work. The data and reports do get through eventually
   OR
3. As the project manager, make a note to seek a one-to-one discussion with the manager right away to resolve the issue and ensure your team get the reports on time.

EMPIRES

A hierarchical organizational structure encourages the development of little empires, where departments have containing walls which can only be breached if you follow specific unwritten rules. This creates an organization with little integration: departmental heads set their own rules making cross-functional coordinated working extremely difficult. Comments like, 'We don't do things that way round here' are common and consistent working practices such as those needed for project work are regarded with considerable mistrust. It is almost like a war zone with missiles thrown at regular intervals to keep the 'enemy' at arm's length and to avoid being blamed when anything goes wrong.

This may sound like an extreme situation but to various degrees it does exist in many organizations. Projects identified as strategic and cross-functional have little real chance of success in such an environment. There are too many opportunities for individuals to attack and sabotage the efforts of a project team. Breaking down the walls or barriers to create an environment for successful cooperation with a common vision is clearly a task for the senior management of the organization. They must want to create an open environment where everyone is clearly focused on a strategic vision.

The consequences of 'empires' for your project are serious. You can find it impossible to reach agreements or even if you do they are frequently ignored and broken. There is little sense of obligation demonstrated and any attempt to create a real sense of good time management is hopeless. Your only course of action is to take the difficulties directly to your project sponsor with clearly illustrated evidence of the impact on the project. A strategic project should have a 'Must not fail' label which all departmental managers must acknowledge. Your sponsor has the authority to cross the boundaries of these empires and create an atmosphere of willing cooperation.

Your project is always vulnerable and all your efforts to encourage good time management and keep the project on track are wasted unless you respond promptly to such issues and escalate them for some very prompt action.

HAVE REGULAR ONE-TO-ONES

Many of the time management problems and their impact can be reduced with quick identification and realization that there is a problem. Performance management is an essential part of your job and this needs regular contact with all your resources and the stakeholders. The one-to-one meetings with each team member are essential to help you:

❑ demonstrate your concern and interest in their welfare;
❑ understand the individual person;
❑ learn about their experience, skills, interests, beliefs, aspirations and how they feel about their work;

❑ learn what concerns they have about their work, problems they have with the work itself, and any difficulties they have with managing their time effectively;
❑ agree personal targets aligned to the plan;
❑ monitor and discuss performance;
❑ identify areas for future training and development;
❑ agree any relevant recommendations to pass to their line manager.

The meetings are informal but actions agreed are recorded and reviewed in the next discussion. Allow 30 to 45 minutes for each meeting and decide a frequency at the start of the project. Usually a monthly meeting is adequate but it does depend on the length of the project. Meetings of this type never prevent ad hoc discussions and do not take the place of regular monitoring activities.

You have close and detailed information about each team member's performance and this needs to be passed back to their line manager as part of the more formalized performance appraisal process. You can only make an objective contribution to this process through having a regular dialogue with each team member. A subsequent poor or indifferent appraisal review interview may be blamed on you, with a serious impact on an individual's motivation!

Remember that you need a similar regular dialogue with your project sponsor to sustain your own motivation to achieve success.

Steps to Improve

1. Establish good relationships with stakeholders, particularly resource managers.
2. Monitor regularly – don't assume it is all happening.
3. Encourage your team to prioritize their work in line with the project schedule.
4. Set personal targets for team members.
5. Reinforce feedback processes.
6. Hold regular one-to-ones with the team.

14

CLOSING YOUR PROJECT

All good things must end – even your project as it passes into company history! You have overcome the trials and tribulations of the issues that seemed like 'mission impossible' at the time, to enter the final phase of your project. Many issues can still arise and you must continue to monitor carefully to ensure a successful outcome. Closure of a project does not just happen: you must plan it with care.

Ensure your communication processes keep the sponsor and other management involved right up to the celebration of completion. The last thing you want is to become infected with a common virus – 'project drift'.

WHAT IS PROJECT DRIFT?

This occurs when you relax the control system and allow the customer or other stakeholder to throw in a few add-ons: 'Just before you finish the project will you have a look at this modification?' Late changes of mind add significant extra work and considerable costs to the project.

As the project nears completion everyone will be concerned about their next assignment and this may show in reduced motivation with a slowing down of effort and lack of commitment. You must keep the momentum going and avoid losing team members to other projects or operational activities.

The users will be anticipating the hand over and may attempt to advance the completion by taking short-cuts. If the changes the users have to accept at hand over are still not popular or accepted, they may obstruct completion and create additional work to cause delays.

CASE STUDY – SCENARIO 13

You are entering the final phase of the project with six weeks to the completion day. Alison informs you her manager has offered her an opportunity to be the project manager of a new project set to kick off in two weeks. She is excited about her first real increase in responsibility in her ten years with the company. Alison has come to you and asked to be released from your project. Should you:

1. Call a team meeting immediately, tell them the situation and lead a discussion into how this will impact on the project and what solutions they can derive to take on Alison's workload
    OR
2. Have a one-to-one discussion with Alison and stress how important it is for her to stay with your project through to completion. Explain how you think her departure could threaten the project
    OR
    Do you have another option?

HAVE YOU SET THE COMPLETION CRITERIA?

The acceptance process should be part of your plan. This will have included just what completion means to your customer and their user group. Check the specific criteria they want to use to confirm completion. Project completion could be signified by:

❏ all tasks finished;
❏ specific deliverables finished;
❏ testing programmes finished;

❏ training programmes prepared and/or finished;
❏ equipment installed and operating;
❏ documentation manuals finished;
❏ process procedures finished and tested;
❏ staff training finished.

All criteria for completion must be measurable by agreed methods, or conflicts will arise.

THE ACCEPTANCE PROCESS

For most projects it is easy for the team to identify the essential steps of hand over. Establish a checklist which you must agree with your customer and the user group. This checklist includes a list of activities that must be finished before acceptance is confirmed and should include questions about:

unfinished non-critical work	the project tasks done
the deliverables achieved (ie, the customer's criteria)	quality standards attained testing and validation of
installation of equipment/ processes	equipment/processes training of operating staff and
new standard operating procedures	management outstanding issues awaiting
setting up a help desk	resolution
identifying follow-on projects	limits of acceptability.

The acceptance process should also identify the customer representative who has the authority to sign the project completion report.

In addition, confirm:

❏ who is responsible for each step of the acceptance process and the work involved;
❏ what post-project support is required and who is responsible;
❏ what post-project support can be available;
❏ for how long such support must be given.

Once an agreed process is produced with a hand over checklist, you are ready to implement the final stages of the project.

SET UP A CLOSE-OUT MEETING

Prepare the team well for this important meeting – carry out a full and rigorous review of the project status.

Check that all work is finishing on time and that there are no forgotten tasks. At this stage it is quite common to find a number of outstanding minor tasks from earlier key stages still unfinished. They are not critical and have not impeded progress, yet they must be completed. Agree action plans to complete all these tasks soon to avoid giving your customer an excuse to withhold acceptance.

Focus on outstanding issues and allocate responsibility for each with clear target dates for resolution. When you are satisfied that everything is under control, confirm the date of the close-out meeting with your customer and the project sponsor. At this meeting you:

❏ review the project results achieved;
❏ go through the hand over checklist;
❏ confirm and explain action plans for any outstanding work or issues;
❏ agree and confirm responsibilities for any ongoing work or support;
❏ confirm who is responsible for monitoring project benefits;
❏ thank the team and stakeholders for their efforts and support;
❏ thank the customer and your project sponsor for their support and commitment.

Provided you have done everything the hand over checklist demands, acceptance should be agreed and the completion report approved and signed. You can then evaluate the project before finally closing the file for good.

EVALUATION

Evaluation is the process used to review the project and identify what went well and what went badly. You then need to ask, 'Why?'

You need to evaluate the technical work, achievements, the project processes and the management of the project.

Evaluation is difficult to complete because everyone who has been involved in the project is looking to their next assignment. People do not want to be reminded of what went badly and to start an inquest at this late stage. You should treat evaluation as an opportunity to learn, not to create blame for what didn't go well.

Active evaluation

An effective project team is always keen to learn from what they are doing. Promote evaluation by encouraging the team to question the way they carry out the project work. This is particularly valid when issues are resolved by asking relevant questions.

There are no rules for evaluation – just let the team focus on identifying opportunities for learning. This is continuous improvement in action, leading to better ways of doing things. What is more important is that anything learned must be accepted and broadcast so everyone can benefit from the experience.

Post-project evaluation

Valuable experience and information are gained during a project. Much of this is lost in project archives and never recovered to help future project teams. Lessons learned during a project should be documented and distributed to individuals engaged or likely to be engaged in project activities. Opportunities for improving processes and procedures are continually present.

It is useful to carry out post-project evaluation asking in-depth and searching questions about each dimension of the project manager's role:

❏ managing the project stakeholders;
❏ managing the project life-cycle;
❏ managing the performance of the stakeholders, yourself and the team.

Asking questions about the project leads to further questions of cause and effect; these should be addressed by the project team as a means of checking that all possible learning points are identified. The results of this evaluation should be published in the post-project report. It is tempting to avoid those things that went wrong because of the risk of hurting someone's feelings. If it involves senior management it may be perceived as direct criticism and career-limiting! Focus on facts, not perceptions and avoid negative statements. Remember the purpose of this whole process is to learn.

Technical evaluation

The technical evaluation is concerned to demonstrate that the best results were obtained with the skills, experience and technology available to you throughout the project. You need to focus the team on identifying:

❏ where successes were achieved;
❏ where technical problems occurred;
❏ how creativity was encouraged during the project.

Much can be learned from this evaluation that is fundamental to the growth of knowledge in the organization.

It is important to recognize that your technical achievements may have a value to others, often far more than you can realize at the current time. Do ensure that the technical part of your

evaluation report is distributed to anyone who could benefit
from your efforts. The information you gather through evaluation must be shared widely if the organization is to realize the
maximum benefits from your efforts. You will similarly learn
from the efforts of your colleagues with other projects.

POST-PROJECT APPRAISALS

At some stage after the project hand over the project benefits
should be measured. The benefits of the project are not all
immediately apparent. At the definition phase of the project you
set out the project benefits; these are likely to be concerned
with:

❑ generating improvements in equipment and plant performance;
❑ creating new income from a new product introduction;
❑ improved efficiency from re-engineering processes and
   procedures;
❑ increased effectiveness from skills enhancement by training
   programmes.

All of these benefits can be quantified and measured by agreed
metrics. Compare these results with any cost-benefit analysis
carried out at the start of the project. At the closure of the
project, agree who is responsible for the measurement of
benefits and when they are to be reviewed. If the project has
produced a successful outcome, you will almost certainly want
an involvement, even if it only means getting regular reports
over the next 12 months.

When the benefits accumulate later, give the team members
some feedback – they will be interested.

CASE STUDY – SCENARIO 14

So your project has finally reached hand over point. The team feel justifiably pleased with the results and the customer seems to be happy. You know there is one final thing to do: evaluate the work done and produce a final report. This could lead to more projects for you and the team, so you:

1. Tell the team they have done a great job and there is now one task remaining. Ask them to meet and evaluate the project and then agree the outline, structure and contents of the final report
    OR
2. Call a team meeting and conduct a structured evaluation, then explain the structure of the report and assign tasks for individual sections to the team members. The final report should reflect on your leadership ability and everyone's performance
    OR
    Do you have another option?

AND FOR MY NEXT TRICK. . .

You have finished the project, delighted your customer and issued your evaluation in a final report. Now you can celebrate with your team – a job well done! Call a celebration team meeting and ask the customer and other stakeholders to come along. Ask your project sponsor to address the group and put on record the success achieved. After the euphoria of this celebration, remember to make sure your project file is completely updated before you close it for the last time!

But what comes next? Perhaps another project, promotion or just back to operational activities? Ask yourself:

❑ what you have gained from the experience of managing the project;
❑ what actions you can take to improve your performance even more.

Every project is unique and your continued development comes from this self-analysis that will lead you on to greater success in the future. Develop the skills of project management further for the larger projects that are becoming part of working life in most organizations today, and continue to enjoy the experience.

Steps to Improve

1. Watch out for project drift.
2. Derive an agreed acceptance process.
3. Hold a close-out meeting with your customer.
4. Celebrate the project completion.
5. Evaluate to learn, not blame.
6. Analyse your performance.
7. Ask your sponsor for feedback.
8. Analyse the team's performance and reward them.

APPENDIX 1

CASE STUDY COMMENTARY

SCENARIO 1

This is the first time the team meets together, so it is premature to start seeking ideas and suggestions. Similarly the team should not focus on technical details until they have a clear understanding of the project's overall objectives. You do not yet have a clear understanding of all the customer's needs. At this stage of the project it is important that everyone understands the project context, the overall objectives and how you see these being achieved. Focus the team on the general processes you believe necessary and share your enthusiasm and commitment to the project.

SCENARIO 2

A common situation you will meet. You cannot ignore the information and you cannot divert the team away from your project so early. Although you can approach the second prospective customer direct, it is possible this manager may have started a project in their department and is your competitor. There are likely to be others who will have some interest in your project so it is appropriate at this stage to send a memo to all managers, informing them about your project and giving them an opportunity to respond with their interests. This is really the responsibility of the project sponsor.

SCENARIO 3

Risk assessment is only effective if everyone participates to share experience and judgement. You should not ignore the negative opinions expressed as this can affect others in the team. Focus the team on the challenge and stress that the whole point of the activity is to identify how to minimize the impact of risks. Emphasize your confidence that these risks can be overcome if everyone is aware of their existence and watches out for the triggers that indicate a risk is likely to happen. If the negativity persists then you can discuss this with the team member in your next one-to-one.

SCENARIO 4

Graham is very experienced but you cannot expect to get the best plan from just one viewpoint. If you set his plan aside, Graham may feel you are not recognizing his efforts and he is demeaned before the team. Asking each team member to develop their own version takes a long time to agree an acceptable plan with all the team. Use Graham's efforts as the starting point for planning and after reviewing the plan Graham may accept that he has left out some activities. It is important to involve all the team in planning and avoid too much detail at the first stages of the process. Allowing team members to take a lead role is acceptable when justified by their expertise. You must always take back the leadership at the appropriate point and ensure everyone is focused on the project objectives.

SCENARIO 5

There is no substitute for good teamwork in planning. If there are problems of scheduling you must be involved yourself. Just giving the team ideas suggests you want to stand away from the day-to-day detail. They need help and in the interest of time you cannot leave them to eventually come up with an answer. This will lead to you issuing an edict for the schedules and they will adopt a 'hands-off' position, saying the schedules are unrealistic and not achievable. You must facilitate the planning yourself using their knowledge and skills to derive schedules that are realistic and accepted by everyone.

SCENARIO 6

Performance in the organization is everyone's responsibility. You cannot push the request back to the manager and say it is not your job. You do not have regular contact with these team members so you cannot comment accurately on their performance. Although the team could discuss these evaluations it will take time and could lead to conflict. Performance is a personal matter between individual and supervisor, so give the responsibility to the key stage owners to assess the performance of all the team members reporting to them. Your key stage owners are responsible for the detailed control of the work in their key stage and must be the best people to comment on the performance of those doing this work. You can then ensure these reports are objective. This emphasizes good teamwork.

SCENARIO 7

The customer has called the meeting, so how can the team prepare an agenda? Requests for increased productivity may have a short-term benefit. The team may feel this is just painting the surface to look good. Good leadership is essential here to prepare the ground. Get all status reports up to date and ensure all project documentation is accurate. You are then fully prepared for anything that comes up at the meeting. You must ask the customer for the agenda to be sent through in advance of the meeting to allow good preparation.

SCENARIO 8

'Increasing productivity is never easy to achieve quickly. The team will probably debate this issue endlessly – just wasting time. You could ignore the slippage until the next one occurs! Unfortunately projects slip a day at a time. One day soon becomes five days and this soon becomes five weeks. Demonstrate your leadership through effective action planning to find a solution to maintain the original schedule. Treat any slippage as a crisis – remember you have made a commitment to your customer and you are obliged to do everything possible to maintain the completion dates.

SCENARIO 9

However hard you try, it is difficult to hide such information. The grapevine is always very effective! If you ignore it, the team will certainly hear of the possibility of cancellation and expect you to say something. It is better to share the information and focus the team on maintaining current workloads. Involve the team in the assessment of the risks and consequences. When meeting your customer it could force a change of mind.

SCENARIO 10

You cannot just leave this issue to resolve itself. It happens all the time in project work and this type of conflict can be difficult to manage.

Your team expect you to look after their interests and support them. The line managers are important stakeholders and it is your responsibility to have dialogues with them to understand their interests. You should meet with them and try to reach a compromise, if necessary involving your sponsor to give additional support. If the team have been too aggressive in their scheduling, the project will have an excessively high level of risk.

SCENARIO 11

If one of the team is not performing the rest will know and for a while may carry the workload. However, they may also feel frustrated that you have not apparently noticed. Asking the team to improve productivity again may appear to them as if you are either blind or ignoring the issue. They cannot resolve your problems for you. Performance issues are your responsibility and you should have a one-to-one discussion with Ian and try to improve his performance, setting some personal targets for his project work. If appropriate, also involve his line manager in a further discussion.

SCENARIO 12

You are now clearly aware of the issue and cannot ignore the request by the team for support. They expect you to do something to improve information flow. Ignoring the problem only adds to their frustration, so you must seek a meeting with the manager to try and find a better way to speed up the information flow. If there is no agreement then you must use the issue escalation process to take this to your sponsor. This could create additional problems, possibly near open warfare, but it is important in the interest of the project to ensure this manager clearly understands the reasons for your concerns.

SCENARIO 13

Once someone has been offered another opportunity it is very difficult to ask them to reject it. Alison is excited at being offered her real chance at last. She may consider your attempts to block her transfer as interfering with her personal development. This is not motivating her and will lead to conflict. The team will probably feel that she should grab this rare opportunity, while at the same time feeling some concern for the consequences for the project. A good team will pull together to resolve the workload

problem, asking you to seek some additional resource support
to complete the project. You could try and delay the start-up of
the new project and keep Alison in your team to the completion
date.

SCENARIO 14

The evaluation process and final report are your responsibility
and you should set out the structure of this report. Assign tasks
so that each team member can report on their part of the project.
Agree with the team the performance issues to be included in
the report. The appearance and content of this report will
always reflect on your leadership ability and team performance.
A poor report may be career-limiting; a good one benefits
everyone.

ANALYSING THE LOGIC DIAGRAM

The logic diagram you have derived is the core of the planning process. It shows all the relationships between the activities you have identified as essential to achieving the project objectives. The steps involved in analysing this diagram are simple. With more activities the diagram becomes increasingly complex, so before attempting to carry out the calculations, review the diagram.

TIDY UP THE LAYOUT

Make sure all arrows showing dependency are clearly marked, entering an activity on the left-hand side of the card and exiting an activity on the right-hand side of the card.

Try to arrange the cards so that arrows do not cross each other – this can cause confusion. If it cannot be avoided, use connectors:

VALIDATE THE LOGIC

Finally, before proceeding, validate the logic by asking the same questions about dependency, only this time work backwards from finish to the start. This often uncovers:

Dangles – activities with no entry or exit dependency, which is not logical. Every activity must have both for continuity.

Loops – activities with a reverse dependency, creating a loop which is infinite work! Break any loops and question the dependencies again.

Then proceed with the analysis as shown on pages 152–154.

STEP 1
Decide the time each activity or key stage will take and enter these durations on to the logic notes or boxes.

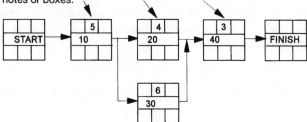

STEP 2
Number each box from start through to finish, working from left to right – numbers or alphanumerics.

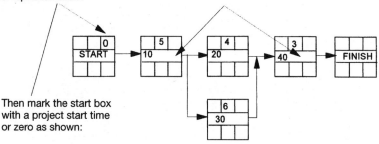

Then mark the start box
with a project start time
or zero as shown:

STEP 3
Transfer this time figure to the next box in the logic diagram:

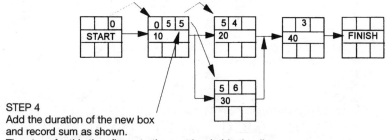

STEP 4
Add the duration of the new box
and record sum as shown.
Then transfer this time figure to the next box(es) in the diagram.

STEP 5
Repeat step 4 working through the logic diagram from left to right.
When `paths' meet, ensure you record the highest number into the next box.

The completed forward pass analysis now looks like this:

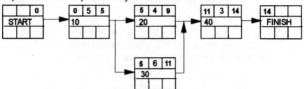

From this we can conclude that the earliest time this small project can finish is 14 units of time.   The whole process is now reversed.

STEP 6
Transfer the finish time to the bottom corner of the box as shown.

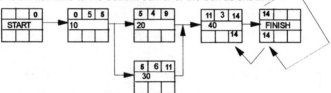

Then copy this same time figure to the lower right-hand corner of the predecessor box.

STEP 7
Subtract the activity duration from this time figure and enter the result in the lower left-hand corner of the same box.

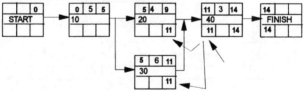

Then copy the result time figure to the lower right-hand corner of any predecessor boxes as shown.

STEP 8
Continue step 7, copying the lowest time figure to the next predecessor box where paths merge in the reverse pass.

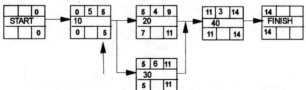

The analysis of this logic diagram is now complete and the critical elements can be clearly defined.

STEP 9
Look at each box in turn and identify those where the difference between the time figures in the upper and lower left-hand corners is equal to the difference between the time figures in the upper and lower right-hand corners.

These boxes in your diagram are the critical elements
and form the critical path of the logic diagram.

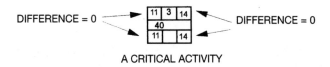

A CRITICAL ACTIVITY

STEP 10
Finally enter the above calculated difference in the lower middle part of the box. This is the spare time or float time.

Then calculate the float times for all the boxes in the diagram:

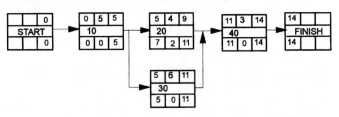

The logic diagram analysis is now complete. Record the data in tabular format.

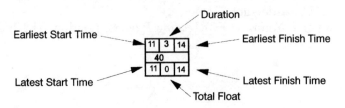

APPENDIX 3

FURTHER READING

Alan Barker (1993) *Making Meetings Work*, London, The Industrial Society.

John Crawley (1992) *Constructive Conflict Management*, London, Nicholas Brealey.

Jenny Davenport and Gordon Lipton (1993) *Communications for Managers*, London, The Industrial Society.

Rupert Eales-White (1992) *The Power of Persuasion*, London, Kogan Page.

J Davidson Frame (1994) *The New Project Management*, San Francisco, Jossey-Bass.

Herbert S Kindler (1990) *Risk Taking*, London, Kogan Page.

Keith Lockyer (1984) *Critical Path Analysis and Other Project Network Techniques*, London, Pitman.

S Pokras (1989) *Successful Problem Solving and Decision Taking*, London, Kogan Page.

M D Rosenau (1992) *Successful Project Management*, New York, Van Nostrand Reinhold.

Martin Scott (1992) *Time Management*, London, Sunday Times/ Century Business.

Dorothy M Stewart (editor) (1992) *Handbook of Management Skills*, Aldershot, Gower.

Trevor L Young (1993) *Leading Projects*, London, The Industrial Society.

INDEX